Digging for
DIAMONDS

'Cathy Madavan is a skilled communicator who writes with a pace and sparkle that simply draws you in. Dip into this book at random and I promise you you'll find yourself reading the whole thing! As you will learn, Cathy's positive outlook on life has not come from living on easy street. Her adventures have taken her to deep mines and through dark passages. It is from both the highs and the lows that she brings out here, with such freshness, the kinds of gems you can really do something with.'

Gerard Kelly
Writer, preacher-poet, founder of The Bless Network

'Disarmingly funny one moment, pointedly wise the next, *Digging for Diamonds* is full of warmth, wit and honesty. Sometimes the finest treasures are buried deep, and Cathy Madavan shows us where the gems lie by revealing some of her own precious finds.'

Sheridan Voysey
Writer, speaker, broadcaster, and
author of *Resurrection Year:*
Turning Broken Dreams into New Beginnings

'I loved reading *Digging for Diamonds* – and I think you will too. Some writers have the skill to be able to articulate thoughts, fears, hope and dreams in a way that makes us sigh and whisper, "That is exactly how I feel – it's as if she knows me." Cathy Madavan has that skill – and not just because she is a wonderful writer but because she allows us into the secret place of her own life, and in doing so unlocks the door to our own. And if she is right then we are richer than we dare imagine – if only we can discover the treasure within. A rare and lovely book.'

Rob Parsons, OBE
Author and founder of Care for the Family

'Cathy Madavan's words are beautiful. As I read them, I had the sense that God was pushing his hands into my life and extracting jewels of hope, purpose and meaning. *Digging for Diamonds* is a rare gem. It's like a prism that displays God's love and grace in awe-inspiring, jaw-dropping wonder. Don't just read this book, ponder it and let it refract into your heart. You'll be brought closer to Jesus, as his love is made clearer to you.'

Malcolm Duncan
Pastor at Gold Hill Baptist Church,
and chairman of the Spring Harvest planning group

'I've never been a polish-my-jewellery type of girl, but finding time to read this book has been like adorning my soul. Cathy's biblical wisdom, her honest stories and deep questions have buffed me to a shine. Invest!'

Abby Guinness
Spring Harvest Event Director

'Honest, challenging and fun. *Digging for Diamonds* will prompt you to take a look at some of the issues in life that many of us keep well hidden. Cathy writes with humour and a disarming honesty that touches the heart. A great read.'

Katharine Hill
UK Director, Care for the Family

'This is a book to read, re-read and then pass on to your friends and family. It's a book full of warmth and humour and brimming with the kind of wisdom that gets you up in the morning to face a difficult new day. Knowing your worth, your true value in God and to God, is one of the greatest gifts of all, enabling you to navigate the obstacles that life places in your path with confidence. Cathy takes us on an incredible journey to discover what being God's masterpiece really means.'

Bekah Legg
Editor, *Liberti* magazine

'Cathy is part of the growing breed of Christian influencers who are using their blessed normality, yes normality, to reach people. She is mind-blowingly refreshing. No spiritual airs or hierarchical graces – just astounding honesty, integrity and wisdom. In *Digging for Diamonds*, Cathy uses the day-to-day encounters of her life to share profound truth as to our value and worth. She does this with laugh-out-loud humour and sparkling wit. This is a book that should sit on the kitchen table, not the book shelf, close at hand, to be picked up again and again, read to each other, absorbed, shared, reflected on and cherished.'

Tania Bright-Cook
Chair of Love146 Europe, speaker, author, spiritual director, CEO – Bright Cook Consultancy

'Cathy Madavan is the epitome of someone who has dug for treasure and has rejoiced in the gems she has discovered. I have known Cathy for many years now and have watched her remain joyful and hopeful in the challenges of her life as a wife, mother, leader and businesswoman. Her ability to communicate empowers us all to enjoy the gems she has found, which in turn enables us to dig for our own inner treasure. As we all know, the world is full of fairly competent people but it is people with character and wisdom where the resources are depleted. Investing in digging deeper with Cathy will inspire you to become the person God intended you to be. I highly recommend it!'

Vicky Taylor
Founder of Free Range Chicks,
leadership consultant, trainer and coach

'Cathy Madavan is a "once met never forgotten" kind of person. I can still remember the day she introduced herself to me as a brand-new follower of Christ, on her first day in our church. Over the years I have watched Cathy grow in God as a disciple, wife, mother and leader. This honest, practical and realistic book helps explain how we can all grow to be the people God intends us to be. Read it and realise your potential in Christ.'

Revd Ian Coffey
Vice Principal & Director of Leadership Training,
Moorlands College, author and speaker

'I'm applying for the role of President of the Cathy Madavan Fan Club. She is hilarious! In a frank, humorous and incredibly insightful way, Cathy has hit multiple nails on . . . well, multiple heads. She has the capacity to address some really serious issues Christian women face in and outside the church in a light-hearted and very amusing way.

We get so sick of reading and hearing the polished-up version of people's stories. *Digging for Diamonds* takes a holistic approach to life and spirituality, for women every-where, bringing wisdom, grace and enabling them to under-stand who they are in Christ.

Full of wry humour and witty observations, it's the book that needed to be written. Give it to your mum, your sister, your best friend – or your worst enemy. You won't be sorry, and neither will they. One of the top books for women this year. The guys will like it too.'

Bev Murrill
Speaker, author, leadership consultant,
Director – Christian Growth International, UK

'Cathy Madavan may not have discovered a new land-mass or spotted a rare species of tropical fauna, but she is a great explorer! She has succeeded in plumbing the depths of the complex waters of the human heart and mind with page-turning honesty, humility and LOL humour. By uncovering her own life-quakes and quests in her pursuit to understand true value and divine potential, she very naturally uncovers ours and leads us bold and smiling into a world of discovery.'

Sue Rinaldi
Writer, speaker, musician and creative consultant

Digging for
DIAMONDS

Finding treasure in the
messiness of life

Cathy Madavan

Authentic

Reprinted 2016

21 20 19 18 17 16   8 7 6 5 4 3

First published 2015 by Authentic Media Limited,
PO Box 6326, Bletchley, Milton Keynes, MK1 9G.
authenticmedia.co.uk

British Library Cataloguing in Publication Data
A catalogue record for this book is available from the British Library.

ISBN 978-1-78078-131-0
ISBN 978-1-78078-247-8 (e-book)

Cover design by Tina Grobler, Pegasus Graphics (pegasusgraphics.co.uk).
Printed and bound in Great Britain by CPI Group (UK) Ltd, Croydon, CR0 4YY.

CONTENTS

PURPOSE   161

ACKNOWLEDGEMENTS

While writing a book is an undeniably solitary sport, it is also, it turns out, impossible without a team.

So I would like to thank my team for being amazing. I hope and pray they will know how appreciated they are – and that this book would have been impossible without them. (This is like an Oscars ceremony – I might just pop on a posh frock and get emotional!)

Firstly, I would like to express my massive thanks to Mark, Naomi and Izzy who learned to live with a middle-aged woman who, though she was physically present, was to all intents and purposes distracted, grumpy and continually muttering about carbon allotropes. This would be hard for any family to bear. And while you escaped a few music practices and didn't miss my nagging about cleaning the house, you also paid a high price as I stared at my laptop. Thank you, fabulous family, for allowing me to write this book – it is as much for you as for anybody.

Also, I really thank God for some special cheerleaders in my life. Where would I be without the likes of Bev Murrill, Rob and Di Parsons, Sheridan and Merryn Voysey,

Diane Louise Jordan, Sue Rinaldi, Roger Hulbert, Abby Guinness, Bekah Legg, Celia Bowring, Vicky Taylor, Malcolm Duncan, Gerard Kelly, Katharine Hill, Ruth Fletcher, Tania Bright-Cook, the Locks Heath Free Church tribe and the vital and timely delivery of cupcakes from Katie Scott? Those texts, Facebook comments, feedback and prayers were my lifeline, and those cakes were delicious.

But there are two people who deserve a special mention. Tina Grobler, you are a woman of immense graphic-design skill, photography smarts and computer wizardry but you also possess the patience of a saint. How many hours did it take us to find a design that worked? And how many fonts?! You are amazing. And last, but absolutely by no means least, I cannot thank enough Amy Boucher Pye. Without her I would still be waffling away about book ideas, with little chance of actually getting it done. You are more than an editor, Amy, you have been my instigator, my motivator, my prayer warrior, my encourager and my giant nag. Most of all, you have become a special and trusted friend. Thank you for making it happen.

I thank God for his insight and encouragement, for the wonderful Authentic team, for every person who stood with me and for every reader who delves into these pages. We're all in it together, after all. What a team!

FOREWORD

Eighteen months ago, I made friends with a young man who had been raised in a tough part of South London and had certainly started life on the wrong side of the tracks. Growing up he never knew his father and because his young mother struggled to parent him on her own, from the age of 2 his childhood was spent flitting between care homes and foster families. By the age of 7 his anger was so uncontrollable that the local primary school excluded him. And by the time he became a teenager his life had been written off. Teachers and foster parents alike didn't really believe he'd come to much.

Yet despite the chaotic nature of his upbringing my young friend harboured a seriously unrealistic desire to study at Cambridge University. No one in his school had ever achieved this, let alone a young lad who'd spent most of his time in detention, narrowly avoiding further exclusion.

But somehow (possibly spurred on by his new found faith at the age of 14) he achieved his ambition, and after three years of disciplined study left Fitzwarren College, Cambridge with a strong upper second degree in History, which has in turn opened doors to many more opportunities for him.

Now I don't know to what extent his new found trust in God affected the dramatic transformation in his fortunes, but I am reminded of these words of scripture: 'His divine power has given us everything we need for a godly life through our knowledge of him who called us by his own glory and goodness' (2 Pet. 1:3).

My young friend's story reaffirms my strong belief that everyone is great. None of us, even those of us born in the most distressing of circumstances, is an accident. We're not a mistake! In fact we are all astonishing beyond measure.

Sadly though, unlike my young friend, too many of us spend most of our lives never truly believing that, never tapping into our greatness, never really acknowledging our true *innate* worth.

Alarmingly, this applies to most of us, whether we're obviously struggling with life or we appear to be incredibly successful. Through the diverse nature of my work I've come into contact with a wide variety of people. I've had the opportunity to work with top business men and women in prestigious organisations. Some, contrary to their obvious outward success, have revealed to me their deep sense of failure or anxiety about their performance. Likewise, I have known exhausted parents, running to keep still, who wonder if anybody truly notices who they are or what they do. It would seem that the issues of self-esteem and self-acceptance are close to many of our hearts. However polished we may appear to be, scratch the surface and far too many of us feel inadequate and overlooked.

Thankfully, in her long-awaited book *Digging for Diamonds*, the brilliant Cathy Madavan assures us that embedded in each one of us is precious raw material waiting to be shaped and stewarded into a purposeful, exceptional life. According to Cathy we are who we are for a reason. As DNA testing proves none of us are the same, even identical twins. We're all unique, with a matchless purpose.

In the pages of this immensely practical book Cathy helps us to see that our lives are not about competition, not about being greater or lesser than anybody else – but first and foremost about being comfortable in our own skin and from that strong foundation intentionally growing in such a way as to make a significant difference, not just for ourselves but for others too.

I first met Cathy a couple of years ago when we were brought together to share the stage on a speaking tour. I was at once drawn to her warm, engaging personality and kooky sense of humour. It was fun at first sight with Cathy; she seriously makes me laugh.

I also admire how she eloquently uses humour, not just for fun, but to cleverly 'translate' difficult ideas. In fact Cathy is a stunning and compelling communicator who's serious about encouraging each and every one of us to unearth our hidden potential. Possessing that winning combination of talent and diligence, together with unflinching commitment, Cathy is certainly a woman with a plan. The wisdom emanating from this book isn't just great theory – she knows from personal experience what it means to face life's challenges. Cathy walks the talk – she's living proof that it is possible to improve your circumstances and she wants to share the good news!

What I think I admire most about Cathy Madavan is her big-spirited generosity. Cathy genuinely cares about people flourishing to their full capacity; she really does want to contribute to improving lives. In this gem of a book Cathy not only warmly inspires us to take pleasure in who we truly are, she also cleverly provides a nuts and bolts, workable aid to help us do so. Which is why I can't recommend *Digging for Diamonds* enough.

Thank you, Cathy! This is the book we've all been waiting for . . .

Diane Louise Jordan
TV and Radio Presenter

INTRODUCTION

I embody the phrase, 'Champagne taste on a beer budget.'

I love nice things, but let's be clear – I also want them at a nice price. I have been known to stalk Internet auction sites and sales in shops, prowling over prospective purchases, only to leap into action as I steal them from my competitors. I even once took a job for four hours a week at a fancy interiors store for the sole purpose of exploiting the staff discount and furnishing my home very nicely, thank you very much. Stacking pots of paint was not exactly the highlight of my week, but buying incredibly expensive rugs that had been returned by customers for a few pounds most definitely was.

Whether we are talking about buying a computer, a cushion or a cornet, I am happy to report that I will get every bit of bang for my buck that I possibly can. Some people, I suppose, might call it an obsession. Other folk might call me cheap. I'd call it gifted.

The problem for an avid bargain hunter like me is that things generally cost more because they are worth their value. Good quality doesn't usually come cheap, ethically sourced is not often a bargain and bespoke is never ever budget.

Wouldn't it be great if every thing that we value in life could also be found quickly and on the cheap? But it never is. You might look for precious wisdom chopped, vacuum packed and heavily discounted, but you won't find it. It would be wonderful if intimacy or trust could be whisked up and served in a moment, but they can't be. How helpful would it be if life-changing forgiveness could be dispensed at the touch of a button on a vending machine? But it is just not possible.

My hope is that in these pages we will dig together to uncover some riches, taking the time to value them in our lives. These are not easily found bargain truths or hastily cobbled-together values, but treasures that are worth look-ing for, and worth cherishing. Proverbs 2:3–5 says it nicely:

> If you call out for insight
>   and cry aloud for understanding,
> and if you look for it as for silver
>   and search for it as for hidden treasure,
> then you will understand the fear of the Lord
>   and find the knowledge of God.

Years ago, when I was working as a full-time-with-no-overtime-stay-at-home-mum (who would 'cry aloud for understanding' for most of the day), I bought a giant glass 'diamond' paperweight; I wanted to use it at an event at our church as we explored how precious we are to God. But as the years have passed and I have stared at that large mineral muse upon my shelf, many new insights or 'facets' have occurred to me. And others have been added as I have heard diamonds referred to in different places at different times, many of which I'll share in this book. As I have asked God for more insight and understanding, I believe he has graciously used these slowly crystallising truths to shape my thinking and to influence the way I approach my daily life.

Perhaps it goes without saying, but the most precious possession that any of us can discover is a relationship with God through Jesus. It is infinitely valuable and has been bought at unimaginable cost. It is incredible to think that this treasure, this steadfast and eternal hope, is found inside each of us, if we are a follower of his. The apostle Paul tells us, 'We have this treasure in jars of clay to show that this all-surpassing power is from God and not from us' (2 Cor. 4:7). We might be a frail and possibly slightly cracked pot, but Christ is alive in us, no matter what challenges we face or how fragile we feel at times. It's worth reminding ourselves again that, as we look beyond the surface and into our more hidden life, we are precious vessels in whom the Spirit of God wants to make his home.

I wish I knew every person who has taken the trouble to read this book but I have no idea who you are, or at which stage of life you find yourself at the moment. However, I know this: some lessons are described as valuable for a reason and some of the most powerful and life-altering lessons you have learned so far have probably come at a very high price.

Digging for DIAMONDS

Digging for diamonds is not always easy, I know. That's one of the reasons it pays to have a robust sense of humour – we might as well have a laugh at some of our mishaps and mistakes, and it doesn't hurt to throw some light into the messy or dark places we may find along the way.

But also, if your experiences are at all like mine, you'll have seasons where your time is so congested or your mind is so distracted that even if gems were scattered all around you, you might not have the energy or focus to notice them, never mind find joy in them. That's certainly true for me. I might sometimes completely forget to be grateful for the many 'jewels' I have already been given in my life. What are the chances, then, that you and I will take the time necessary to dig beneath the surface of life in order to discover more of what might be hidden beneath?

That's what we will be able to do in this book. And it is vital that we do because, as we will discover, what we can't see always shapes what we can see. So, in each chapter we will explore a different facet or characteristic of the gems that can be discovered in all of us: identity, strength, character and purpose. I encourage you to dig deeper by engaging with the questions at the end of each chapter – you might want to grab a notebook or a journal as you discover more about what God might be saying to you. You might be using this book in a small group, which is fantastic. If so, I encourage you to read the chapter before you meet and to make your own notes in preparation for your time of sharing, exploring further and praying together.

It is my prayer that we will excavate some valuable truths together that will reflect right back into our lives. We have been entrusted with the treasures of God's wisdom, and although our lives are often crazy, sometimes difficult and occasionally downright confusing, I believe that Paul is telling us the truth when he says that 'my God will meet all your needs according to the riches of his glory in Christ Jesus' (Philippians 4:19). Sometimes, we just need to dig a bit deeper to find them.

Got your shovel?

IDENTITY

Chapter 1

VALUABLE

The Lord your God has chosen you out of all the peoples on the face of the earth to be his people, his treasured possession.

Deuteronomy 7:6

In 1905, the superintendent of the Premier Mine in South Africa was taking his daily routine inspection of a tunnel, when he saw what he thought was a piece of glass on the wall of the mine. He assumed it was probably a practical joke left for him by the miners but he dislodged it with his pocket knife anyway until, remarkably, he held in his hands what we now know to be the famous Cullinan Diamond.

The whole world buzzed with the news of the discovery of the largest diamond ever found – twice the size of any previous stone – and much of the discussion focused around the huge security operation necessary to transport a gem of this magnitude to England. The steamboat that eventually travelled with a crew of detectives on board and a heavy parcel in the Captain's safe was all, in fact,

3

nothing more than a rather cunning diversionary tactic, as the genuine diamond itself made its way across the globe in a normal parcel, travelling by registered post. The stone, once delivered, was then painstakingly cut over eight months into nine major stones and ninety-six smaller ones, with the largest, known as the Great Star of Africa at 530.2 carats, together with the next in size, the Second Star of Africa, finding their home in the sceptre and the crown of the British Crown Jewels.

Inherently Valuable

If you have ever been to the Tower of London and stood gawping in admiration at these rare and precious stones, you probably have, like me, been totally dazzled by both their beauty and their jaw-dropping value. Some things, like diamonds and gold (and decent plain chocolate) are just inherently valuable. You don't need to add anything to them; they don't need to accomplish anything or to know anybody special to be of innate worth. They are simply, indisputably valuable.

They just are.

For a moment, try and imagine that you are looking into that cabinet full of jewels again, and that as you adjust your focus slightly, you catch the reflection of yourself in the glass. I wonder, after being dazzled by your extreme good looks, how much you would say you are worth? How exactly do we go about valuing ourselves anyway?

Now my husband would have a very good answer if I were to ask him that question. He could tell me exactly down to the penny what he is worth, because he has it meticulously detailed in his most recent life insurance calculations (swears by his spreadsheets, does Mark). But, as brilliant as he may be with numbers, that's not the value I am talking about here. Your 'worth' comprises so much more than merely the price tag attached to your life.

It seems to me that a few people value themselves extremely highly, giving the impression that they are totally indispensable, with confidence oozing out of their every pore. Which is a bit intimidating really. When I talk to these people I find myself babbling and dropping my custard creams down my front. Others though, at the other end of the spectrum, can't shake off the feeling that they are almost disposable, lacking in any sense of worth or purpose and navigating a daily battle with their self-esteem. Which is a devastating state of mind.

While living in a culture that thrives on the image of unattainable success and beauty doesn't exactly help our self-perception, much of our own sense of value is shaped, for better and for worse, by the significant relationships and experiences in our lives. You might have been brought up in a warm cocoon of unconditional love, where you were accepted and secure to be all you can be – or you might have been brought up with the sense that you could not earn the love of anybody, no matter how hard you tried. You may have experienced life-enhancing relationships that have freed you to grow and flourish – or you may have felt limited or lonely.

> Wherever you find yourself at this moment, you are sure to need to know this one vital thing: you are valuable.

Perhaps the reality is that we will all experience many different seasons of life where our sense of worth might grow or diminish. But wherever you find yourself at this moment, you are sure to need to know this one vital thing: you are valuable. Nothing and nobody can change that. You are indisputably and inherently valuable.

You just are.

Strong Foundations

Looking back, I certainly didn't always feel like I was worth a great deal. In fact, while I was at university I suffered an acute bout of the lack-of-value blues. It had been a rocky few years: my parents had divorced, relationships were strained, my exam results had been disappointing and I had taken off to university feeling unsure about why I was where I was and what I would do with my young life. I really could not see any value in myself at all and, more than anything else, I felt alone. That was all until another student invited me to hang out with a random collection of people who called themselves 'the local church'.

Let me be straight with you: visiting an ancient Brethren chapel in Plymouth wasn't exactly my idea of a cool thing to do at the time. I was more into pubs than pews. But those dear people accepted me in a way I had never imagined possible. I was warmly welcomed into noisy late-night board game marathons, walks along the river and family dinners, and day by day I began to experience, through them, the unconditional love of God. I began to know that, as broken as I was, I was valuable.

VALUABLE

In many ways, that little chapel didn't have a lot going for it. It had an organ and a few dozen people, predominantly older, wearing their Sunday best and hats. There was no sign of the latest technology or a highly trained welcome team with matching t-shirts and Colgate grins to connect with visitors. But I'll tell you what they did have. They had plenty of good old-fashioned love, a sincere faith in God and time to care for a slightly unhinged 18-year-old young woman wearing crazy clothes.

You might not realise it but we are all on the welcome team. We all have a role to play in making sure that people experience not only friendliness but genuine friendship, whatever day of the week it is. Isn't it fantastic (and slightly terrifying) that the diverse assortment of people that comprise the church are God's welcome strategy into his family? No church or individual gets it right all of the time but when we do our embrace demonstrates that wherever people are on their journey of faith, there is a God who values them and who welcomes them into their spiritual home.

Interestingly enough, though, the people of that Brethren chapel didn't waste a whole heap of time before recommending that I make the leap towards a large city Baptist church that had a thriving student ministry with lots of other extrovert young women who liked to talk and didn't wear hats. To this day, I've never quite worked out whether that was a self-protection plan on their part or a selfless act of love and care for me. Either way, it worked out really well.

Surrounded by like-minded people and great teaching, I began to understand more about the Christian faith, and realised I didn't need to be constantly trying harder to be good enough for God. He already loved and valued me more highly than I could have ever imagined. I learned that Jesus was prepared to live his life and give his life so that I might gain a new and eternal life, with the Holy Spirit as my guide. How could I not respond to this kind of unconditional love? And so, armed with my baby faith and the patience of others, I began to build a new future upon the bedrock of the everlasting love of my Heavenly Father.

It turns out, however, that new foundations take a while to dig and even longer to set.

I discovered all I will ever need to know about foundations (and rather more besides) a few years ago when we had an extension built onto our house. I was amazed at the depth to which the builders had to dig to create these new subterranean supports. At one point, I began to wonder if they had mixed up their job sheets and mistakenly started excavating a swimming pool instead. I actually became quite attached to the idea of having a plunge pool outside the back door. But I was also genuinely worried that these new mega-footings would cause stress against the rather shallow foundations of our existing hundred-year-old house. The builders, between slurps of sweet tea (what is it with the tea?), patiently explained to me one more time that the key to the stability of the house was the way that the extension was grafted into the original walls. The new building would not simply be rested against the old or effectively bolted onto it; it had to become properly united, so that each structure strengthened the other rather than pulling against it.

God digs deep foundations in our lives. When you need something strong or want to discover something valuable it often involves digging deep, and it can take a while. Despite our feeble attempts to build our esteem upon the shallow base of achievement or approval, God knows that his foundational truths are the only rocks that can permanently underpin our sense of value and give us our strength. It won't work to try and simply bolt our relationship with him onto the existing structure of our lives –

> God knows that his foundational truths are the only rocks that can permanently underpin our sense of value and give us our strength.

that approach will simply cause tension and instability as the two pull against each other. He longs for his love to integrate with us completely, so that all of our life is secure. It might take a bit of extra groundwork to uncover and destabilise some of our old ways of thinking or our negative patterns of behaviour, but Matthew 7:24–27 tells us that as we build our house on the rock of God's word as opposed to the sandy ground of our own efforts, we will always know our value to God. So when the storms of life come, we will have all we need to stay strong.

Added Value

Often, the things we value most highly are those that mean something far more important to us than their actual cost. I wonder what you would say is your most precious possession? Is it a photo album of memories? A family piano? An antique clock? A letter from a child? Some of the things we cherish are instantly recognisable as items of extraordinary value, but the chances are that what matters to us most is the added meaning and value we have ascribed to an item which represents something special to us.

I remember clearly coming home one night to discover we had been burgled. It's not something you ever forget. As I walked into the hallway I became immediately aware of the debris and mess around me: paper, clothes and the contents of my open drawers either scattered around the house or gone. I was young and didn't have much in the way of fine jewellery or exquisite gems but I was devastated nonetheless. I knew that the stereo could be replaced and I could live without a microwave, but the earrings bought for my sixteenth birthday and the watch given to me by my brother could never be replaced. It was not the expense that mattered at all but the added value – the memories and the relationships that they symbolised.

Even a diamond becomes worth far more than its cost when it represents something deeper. As a couple place a ring on her fourth finger as a sign of their love or when a necklace is passed down from generation to generation, the stone itself becomes a powerful symbol of an enduring emotional attachment that is much more profound than mere monetary value.

In the same way, we can't begin to put a value on all we mean to the people in our lives, or the impact we make upon others. As we build memories and share experiences, our lives become inextricably linked with others', creating priceless relationships and adding value to those around us.

On many occasions I have sat in a funeral thanksgiving service, listening to the moving tributes and wishing that the deceased could be there to hear how valuable their life was, in ways that perhaps they could never have imagined. Is it wrong that I have also considered the merits of having my own pre-death thanksgiving service where I can hear my family, friends and colleagues choking back their emotion as they share anecdotes about my extraordinary abilities and my life-changing influence? But what if they didn't? Maybe not then.

Expressing to others how valuable they are to us and to God is really not a hard thing to do. We can add value to people while they are still alive in a hundred acts of kindness and words of encouragement every day. And the impact can be long-lasting.

> Expressing to others how valuable they are to us and to God is really not a hard thing to do.

A few years ago, my husband Mark and I attended a conference where a church pastor from a large and innovative church in California was speaking. After his session, Mark felt it would be good to speak to him and to ask him to pray for us. It was busy, and it was some time before we found him, but we eventually enjoyed a friendly conversation where he asked us lots of questions, including whether we were ever in California. As it happened, we were about to go there on sabbatical. 'Great,' he said. 'Let's meet up.' Mark looked a bit dubious – this guy has a pretty hectic life after all – but we said we would call. And maybe he could pray for us now anyway. You know, just in case.

But that pastor was true to his word. He took the time to bring his family and meet us for an amazing meal in Downtown Disney. We talked and laughed about life and leadership and he refused to let us pay for the food, and even bought toys for our kids. We felt somewhat over-whelmed and asked why he would take the time to hang out with us, some random unknown British couple. He looked as us, smiled and said, 'Everybody is great to me. Or at least, pre-great!' He saw an opportunity to add value and encouragement into the lives of a young couple and he took it. Not surprisingly, we value him and his ministry even more now than we did before.

Is it possible that, like that church leader, we could begin to deliberately notice the potential value that we can add to the people and the projects around us? Perhaps we might even say a prayer at the start of each day along the lines of, 'Lord, how can I show that I value each person I encounter today?' We are surrounded by potentially significant moments, if only we are alert to the opportunities. We might not feel like we have shed-loads of wisdom, award-winning people skills or excess money to share, but God doesn't ask us to share what we don't have. He does, however, ask us to encourage people and to bless them with what we do have. When we acknowledge that we all have something of value to offer to somebody, then we are able to really notice and value those around us and unlock their potential too. We are all pre-great after all.

Self-Assessment

But a pendulum can always swing too far. Understanding how valuable we are is not the same as being narcissistic or embarking on an endless quest for self-gratification. Although we are indeed described as the apple of God's eye (Ps. 17:8), that doesn't mean that we are the centre of the universe! There is a subtle but rather significant difference between self-belief and self-centredness.

In his book *Orthodoxy*, G.K. Chesterton wittily warns us that, 'The men who really believe in themselves are all in lunatic asylums.'[1] Potential insanity aside, is it possible that we sometimes fall into the trap of believing that our workplaces, our families and even our churches should be all working together to meet our own personal needs? As somebody married to a church leader, I can't begin to tell you how surprising it has been over the years to witness the extent to which some people think that the church should somehow revolve around their own personal preferences. Despite the fact that it would be logistically impossible to accommodate everybody's wish-list in a church with more than four members (and even that might be stretching it), you'd sometimes think the minister was just not trying hard enough to pull it off.

[1] G.K. Chesterton, *Orthodoxy*, new edition (London: Hodder & Stoughton, 1998)

But the gospel is not a self-help, self-actualising plan with 7 steps to a more satisfied and amazing you. God does have good plans for us, and he can do more than we can ask or imagine, but it might not always be found in getting everything we want, when we want it. We are valuable, but we are not entitled. In fact John tells us that 'He must increase, but I must decrease' (John 3:30, ESV). As many a preacher has said, this doesn't mean that we should think less of ourselves, but it does mean that we should think of ourselves less. This is, perhaps, one of the greatest challenges we face in the western church at this time, and it flies in the face of our culture. We must choose a perspective that looks first at the greatness of God, and then to our own desires or worries in the light of that greatness and love. With his help, we will find a place of purposeful humility.

On the other hand, too many of us (perhaps particularly women) allow the pendulum to swing too far the other way and undervalue the contribution we are able to make, whether that is at work, in our homes and communities, or further afield. Despite the enormous capacity we have to impact our surroundings, we are sometimes reticent about stepping out and taking a new opportunity or giving our opinions on a subject. Or if we do step out, we perhaps show a lack of persistence, even stepping back again due to our flagging self-belief. Am I the only one who has sat at a table with people I respect, assuming that they are all so much more valuable and qualified than me for the job in hand? I thought not.

Some of us are trapped by a mindset that is habitually grateful for being noticed or included at all. This is clearly not healthy. A far better outlook would be for us to be grateful for the influence and blessing we have already been given, and to remind ourselves one more time that Jesus welcomes everybody to the table. Other

Other people do not have a special permission-slip to contribute that somebody has forgotten to give us.

people do not have a special permission-slip to contribute that somebody has forgotten to give us. And, let's be honest, those other people like their place at the table and, either deliberately or inadvertently, might not always go out of their way to make us feel included. However, with God's help, each of us can walk in the knowledge that we are valuable and that we add value. We have the ability to step out and make things happen for ourselves.

I know this, because my own need for approval was a driving force for a good portion of my life, and probably still is from time to time. I have felt the temptation to be a social chameleon, trying to make a good impression wherever I am and hoping to avoid the criticism that might crush me. I used to expend so much energy on anxious mental gymnastics, worrying that I was not good enough and ruminating over my actions, that I would waste wonderful opportunities, not only to take part in particular projects but even to try new leisure activities or social outings. I just didn't want to look stupid or to fail. Eventually I had to decide whether to let go of some of my ambitions and goals once and for all, or to get over myself. Fortunately, with an occasional prod from my husband and my friends, I am largely trying to get over myself.

I'll confess, I still occasionally experience a huge waft of self-doubt when I am about to speak at an event or meet certain people, and I sometimes need a big warm dose of reassurance (or a kick up the backside) from those who know me best. But on the whole, my modus operandi is now to smile, to step out and to give my best wherever I go. When we know that God values us and that this makes us innately valuable, we won't waste our limited energy trying to avoid fear or conflict. Those challenges will always exist, but we can respond with a confidence that says, 'I can do all this through him who gives me strength' (Phil. 4:13). We are always valuable and we can add value to others.

And that's worth a lot.

DIGGING DEEPER

- Have you ever visited the Crown Jewels or another set of treasures? What impression did they make on you?

- What impact has your upbringing or life experience had on how you value yourself?

- Thinking of your life at the moment, would you say you feel valued for who you are and what you contribute?

- What is your most precious possession and what makes it so meaningful?

- Consider how you could add value to the people you will meet today or this week.

- Do you ever struggle to articulate your own needs and desires? Or do you find it harder to accommodate the needs of others? Why?

- Is there an area in your life where you could step out more confidently today?

Creator God,

I thank you that nothing can separate me from your love.
I thank you that however I may feel, I am always valuable to
you and I am also valuable to others around me. I pray that
I will grow in a deep assurance of my position as your child,
and that I will live in the confidence that comes from that
knowledge. Lord, in your mercy allow me to see more of
you and help me to see others and myself as you do. Thank
you that I can welcome others into your presence and show
them that there is always a place at your table for them.

In the name of Jesus,

Amen

Chapter 2

UNIQUE

Before you were born, I set you apart for a special work.

Jeremiah 1:5, NCV

My family loves a bit of Saturday night talent show nonsense on the television. Most weeks you will find us snuggled up with pizza and a bucketful of armchair expertise, as we witness the astonishing confidence of people who have no idea of the size of their delusion, alongside those rare moments of raw unfinished brilliance as a person's talent is uncovered for the world to see.

But as the contestants are whittled down, round by round, until only a few remain, I can't help but wonder what happens to the many contestants who didn't get through. Are they standing in the queue of another competition somewhere, still convinced of their destiny, or have they finally realised that their real calling is accountancy?

If there was ever to be a 'Gemstone's Got Talent' competition (And why not? 'Darling, you've got what it takes to really shine!'), the startling truth is that a massive 80 per cent of the raw unfinished diamonds would never even make it through the first round. Even though more than 250 tons of ore are blasted, crushed and processed to yield just one carat of rough diamond, only the fortunate 20 per cent of those get chosen to go to bling boot-camp to be cut and polished and worn by an admiring human. It is, at the end of the process, a very small minority of lucky stones that are selected to be set into gold, dangled on a chain or even, incredible as it seems, placed delicately onto Madonna's eyelashes.

It's a harsh world out there.

So what happens to the rest of the diamond discoveries? Are they just discarded from the line – rejected and sent back to the mine to consider their inadequacy? Not at all, as it happens. Although they might not be suitable for a career in jewellery, the talent found in these rocks is almost endless. These are the diamonds that perform the most miraculous tasks every day. Because of their extraordinary properties, some are used in drill bits or for engraving work, some coat files and polish other materials, others are used in microchips and as semi-conductor coatings, or are used as part of precision components for laser optical equipment. Some are even used to shape other diamonds. In fact, with such unique properties and our increasing technological advances in harnessing those properties, diamonds are set to become an increasingly important part of economic trade and continue to provide the basis for many livelihoods around the world.

If I seem a little defensive about the usefulness of these less than sparkly diamonds, it's because I am. The fact of the matter is that all diamonds are made from the same chemical component, and each has the potential to be used in all kinds of wonderful ways. But we often admire the stones that are either the most beautiful, the most spectacular or worth the most money.

Sound familiar at all?

I am, for the sake of an example, made up of exactly the same chemical components as Kate Moss. It's true. I might be marginally less beautiful, ever so slightly shorter and worth a teensy bit less financially speaking, but does this make me less useful? I think not. Is it really only the glamorous and the powerful people who make a difference in the world day by day?

No.

If only we could share this insight with our glossy, celebrity magazine-enamoured culture. If only we could protect our own minds from the endless comparison of our looks and lifestyle with a few shiny high-profile role-models and instead realise our own unique potential to change the world as we meaningfully engage with people every day. It was Mother Teresa who helpfully said, 'Not all of us can do great things. But we can do small things with great love.'

Miraculous Molecules

Did you know that each diamond is absolutely individual? Every diamond has been formed under extreme heat and pressure over an extraordinary amount of time, and is an allotrope (a pure but distinct form) of carbon. In fact, no matter what its size, each one can be considered to be a single molecule. Because of how they are formed, the complex characteristics of each stone will never be duplicated, meaning that no two diamonds can ever be the same and every diamond is endowed with a personality, character and potential uniquely its own.

Every diamond is endowed with a personality, character and potential uniquely its own.

If we can admire the uniqueness of these gemstones and marvel at their properties and the precariousness of their existence, then how much more inspiring are we? We, who are 99 per cent oxygen, carbon, hydrogen, nitrogen, calcium and phosphorus, and need a precise climate and environment to even exist, are walking miracles. When you look at the complexity of conception, incubation and birth, it is pretty mind-blowing that it ever happens at all. Our bodies are ridiculous in their brilliance – which is why we invariably don't notice until some part of ourselves starts misbehaving or dropping off.

I recently heard a radio interview with one of the world's leading scientific researchers into the eye. The interviewer commented that some people use our scientific understanding of the eye, which is an astonishing example of biological complexity, as an example of how science has explained the world, leaving no room for a faith in God. He wondered if she would agree with that assertion. She paused, then said that even after so many years of research she increasingly found the eye to be a miracle. In fact, she said, it was never a surprise to her when on occasion eyes do not work properly. She is, rather, in awe that they ever actually do work, as unfathomably intricate as they are.

This appreciation of how awe-inspiring it is that we are living and breathing at all, can only lead us to a deep thankfulness to God for every day we are alive. It is profound and inspiring to think that each of us, with our own unique hopes and dreams, is engaged in writing our own one-off life story, and that we also have the privilege of sharing the stories of the people we love.

Bespoke Individuals

Think of it: there never has been and never will be another you. You are the only version of you that the world will ever see. Wouldn't it be a terrible waste of you if we never got to see the best of you? As each of us accept that God has not made a mistake in his design of us, and that perhaps he didn't have a snooze when it came to our creation, we can stop striving to be what we are not and embrace who we really are. We might all be made of the same chemical components, but we are each a genuine, designer, bespoke, one-of-a-kind, made for a reason. Sure, not every one of us will be a world-beating scientist, sing well enough to fill Wembley Arena or compete for our nation in the heptathlon, but we can each do 'me' really well.

I will be honest with you: even the word 'heptathlon' makes me reach for the cake tin. Is it that I am lazy and unmotivated (please don't answer) or is it that I have never been suited to sport? I so clearly remember my school days and those darn hurdles that came up past my waist (I am rather on the short side of the hurdle-to-human spectrum) and the voice of my PE teacher, who had been trained at a special boot camp where doctors' receptionists, PE teachers and parking ticket attendants were put through their paces. But even if she had been ever so slightly less like Gordon Ramsay on a bad day, I was never going to excel at sport. I play cards well. I am pretty good at Monopoly. And, if I was pushed to do some exercise, I'll admit, I like the sound of Pilates. They apparently ask you to lie down in Pilates.

I need to remind myself regularly of the advice in the Bible that says, 'Don't compare yourself with others. Each of you must take responsibility for doing the creative best you can with your own life' (Gal. 6:4–5, MSG).

Just because I find certain things difficult, it doesn't mean I have no talent – I'm just wired up differently. I have, for example, a PhD in writing lists. I have online lists, list apps and a collection of paper lists – I can out-list anybody at ten paces. Also, after a few minutes I can start speaking in the accent of the person I am speaking to (albeit in an involuntarily and quite embarrassing way). And there have been slightly more significant moments, when I have been teaching or writing an article where I have almost felt the whisper of God in my ear saying, 'This is your sweet spot. You were born to do this.'

Where do you feel most alive and in your element? Do you love being with people? Could you create or build things all day long? Are you an organisation junkie who has colour-coded everything? Are you fired up about investing into the next generation? Do numbers really add up for you in exciting ways? Does the thought of helping people get you out of bed in the morning?

Of course, life is never going to be about living in our sweet spot 24/7 all year round. Somebody still needs to clean out the plughole in the bath or stack the chairs, and standing in protest declaring that these menial activities are not actually your gift won't win you many friends. Most of us will take a less than ideal job to pay the bills at some point, and all of us should remain open to serving those around us who need a helping hand, even when it's not easy or natural for us to do so.

But something happens as we also purposefully learn to lean in to 'being me'. As we discover more about the unique contribution only we can make, whether at work or in our communities, we begin to dig into a rich vein of productivity and satisfaction. We become fruitful and fulfilled. We are often more efficient and hardworking because we love it and it comes naturally to us.

> Something happens as we also purposefully learn to lean in to 'being me'.

Most of all, we experience the satisfaction of knowing that our own unique personality and skills can make a difference to the world around us.

Mission Possible

One of the many joys of being a parent is having an excuse to watch animated films like *The Incredibles* over and over again. We love that movie. My children quote large chunks of the script, my husband enjoys the subwoofer rumbles and I sing along to the musical score, which I suspect everybody appreciates far more than they let on. The Incredibles are an ordinary family who each have an extra-ordinary super power, but at the start of the film Mr Incredible has lost sight of the super-hero he was born to be. He is comfortable and settled, can only see his limitations, and has a little too much middle-age spread to fit into his super-suit. But through a collision of events, and bound together by love and a shared mission, the whole family are compelled to work together, each using their unique powers in a united effort to defeat evil and to finally make the world a better place. Gripping stuff.

I reckon the apostle Paul would have loved the Incredibles, although I can't prove that categorically. I imagine he would have said, 'Yes folks, this is what I am talking about when I write "Having gifts that differ according to the grace given to us, let us use them" (Rom. 12:6, ESV). This, people, is what it means to all work together like parts of a body, supporting each other.' Paul knew that the church should be the very place where every member of the family is encouraged to use their own unique gifts to serve the greater good (but possibly without super-suits).

I sometimes sit and imagine all that even one local church could do if every member could truly grasp their God-given potential, working together as God designed us to. In our church we banned the word 'rota' a few years ago to encourage everybody to think about their own unique shape and where they felt a passion to be involved, as opposed to ticking a box on another grid. Nobody minds letting a rota down, but we all feel committed to a team of people and a cause we believe in.

We have found that some- We all benefit thing happens as people come from hearing alive and discover their own the unique places of strength and purpose. perspective of They find a new energy in the others around us good times and they can per- severe during the tough times. But also, we all benefit from hearing the unique perspective of others around us who reflect a different aspect of God's unconditional love for the world. I might be passionate about caring for orphans and widows in a developing country, but you might wake up in the morning thinking about how we can more effectively care for the environment. One friend might have a mission to grow their business through generous, fair and godly values while a different friend might feel equally called to walk with teenagers through their most turbulent years. We need each other.

C.S. Lewis once said that the church is a community of people, each of whom is gifted to be able to see a different aspect of God's beauty in a unique way. And as a result of this, all worshippers throughout eternity will be blessed with an aspect of God they would not otherwise have seen.

Exceeding Expectations

The question is, will we give others and ourselves permission to be fully 'me' or will we simply try to reproduce a carbon copy of some other kind of person? There is a word that comes from the printing trade, where a duplicate printing plate can reproduce the same impression again and again. That word is a 'stereotype'. Gradually the idea of a stereotype has entered our language as we repeatedly ascribe characteristics or behaviour to people or cultures, often revealing a certain set of expectations or even a prejudice about them. Perhaps we believe a politician or a footballer will have certain traits or that a woman CEO will behave in a certain way. We may have views about what disabled people are capable of or what people on benefits do with their time. We see people who are different to us and make sense of that difference by reducing them to a well-worn cliché or we paint certain roles in a rose-tinted hue, which we try to reproduce again and again.

I have tried and failed miserably to be a stereotypical pastor's wife (if such a thing exists – I've never met one). I was not genetically predisposed to be a clergy spouse. I met and married Mark, who went from working in finance into church leadership and I have, on many occasions, asked him whether there is any chance that occupational pathway could be reversed.

I think it would be true to say that our church would probably not wax lyrical about my sensitive pastoral care (I have an allergic reaction to ministries needing tissues) and

UNIQUE

I am hardly the picture of a flower-arranging, scone-baking domestic goddess. In fact, cooking remains a strange and dark art that completely mystifies me. My kids know the deal. I clearly remember having people over for a family dinner one day and hearing my young daughter holding a guest back from the pandemonium in the kitchen with the words, 'Just leave Mummy alone. Don't worry, you'll know when the food is ready, because the smoke alarm will go off.' Charming child. And in my defence, it is quite a sensitive smoke alarm.

I don't fit the stereotype well and I am glad about that. But while our increasingly soundbyte culture might organise our knowledge of the world by simplifying and sorting information and people into generalisations, each time we go against the grain we create a subtle but significant cultural shift. We love it when advertisers, who so often rely on easy stereotypes like 'yummy mummies' or 'adventurous men', take the plunge and defy expectations. Many of us have been inspired by the now famous Dove campaign using real women or the Guinness advert where men playing wheelchair basketball all stand from their chairs at the end of the game, apart from their one disabled friend who they were hanging out and playing sport with. Not many adverts aimed at women are about honest appearance, and very few aimed at men are about making good choices and character.

Likewise, we are inspired by people who, despite their position, their background, or the obstacles or expectations they face, find their calling and thrive in it. I think of the busy single mum I know who defied all expect-ations to become a local magistrate, or the well-spoken and highly educated gentleman in our church who, until he died earlier this year, spent hours supporting young men in prison, despite their cultural differences.

Whether at church, at home or at work, we each have to decide whether we will step out of the shadows to enhance and polish our own unique potential or whether we leave it to become dull or dusty. We are each the man-ager of the resources God has given us to steward in our lives, and we all have to ask our-selves what we are prepared to change in order to grow beyond the expectations of others (or our-selves) into all we can be. We are not called to reproduce a nice or a glossy Christian stereotype any more than we are to be constricted by any limitations oth-ers might place upon us. We are to be a vibrant, risk-taking and radical collection of people who have embraced our own unique calling as disciples of Jesus wherever we are.

We are each the manager of the resources God has given us to steward in our lives.

Climate Change

I remember hearing somebody say that if you want to grow something you have to create the right climate for it. If you want fruit, you have to create a climate for fruit. Likewise, if we want people to grow to be strong and healthy, where they can blossom and be fruitful and fulfilled, then we need to intentionally create a climate where that can happen.

It is, in my experience, in a climate where we are both encouraged and challenged that we grow the strongest. Encouragement alone leaves us weak and prone to storm damage, and challenge alone leaves us stunted and ashamed. But when these two elements work together, we create a climate where we grow strong and tall in our faith, our self-awareness and our sense of purpose.

I am so grateful for the significant people who have nudged me, praised my efforts and corrected my course over the years. I think of people like my first church minister who asked me to speak and read at services and the friends who have dispensed endless wisdom about marriage and ministry over the years. I am so grateful for the way that they have helped to shape the raw material of my life so that I could grow increasingly confident about how God has made me to be.

We all need to proactively create a climate of growth in our own lives where God can prune us and shape us to grow in a healthy direction. But we are not destined to grow in order to just benefit ourselves – we are all uniquely placed to give support, encouragement and opportunity for others to also grow stronger and flourish in their own way.

Whether what we have to offer others is great or small in our eyes, it matters to God. Nobody is insignificant to him and we have all been given a unique personality, skills, experiences, gifts and an area of influence. 'Each of you should use whatever gift you have received to serve others, as faithful stewards of God's grace in its various forms' (1 Pet. 4:10). The amazing thing is that as we invest our time, our talents and our energy wisely in serving others, God so often multiplies it and gives us more back in return than we had anticipated.

There is no sweeter thing than knowing God's pleasure as you fulfil his purposes in a way that only you can do. It might mean taking some risks. It could involve some big decisions. It will probably mean some hard work. But most of all, it will be a daily choice to confidently polish the potential of the unique 'you' that you are designed to be.

DIGGING DEEPER

- Consider for a moment that every diamond is unique. Now reflect upon the fact that each and every person is completely individual, and let that soak in.

- How does our society choose its role models? How do we celebrate more of the less sparkly but equally inspirational role models in our communities?

- What can you do to 'take responsibility for doing the creative best you can with your own life' (Gal. 6:4–5, MSG)?

- What would you say you are born to do? Where do you feel most alive or fulfilled?

- Are there any steps you could take to lean further into the unique gifts and passions that you have? In work, in ministry or in your relationships?

- Have you ever felt constricted by stereotyping or the expectations of others? How can you help yourself and others to break through those limitations?

- How can you create a climate of growth – for yourself and the others in your life?

Heavenly Father,

I thank you that you have plans for me that only I can fulfil. I thank you for the tapestry of my life – my experiences, my passion, my skills and my gifts – and pray that I will steward all you have given me and create a climate where I can grow to serve you and others more fully in a way that gives glory to you and your endless grace. Help me to overcome any obstacles that might hold me back and to have confidence in your unique plans for my life.

I ask these things in the name of Jesus,

Amen

Chapter 3

CREATED

So God created mankind in his own image, in the image of
God he created them; male and female he created them.

Genesis 1:27

Is it just me, or is watching an artist go about their business
an extraordinary and mysterious experience? How do they
know where to put what colour? What are they seeing in
their mind's eye as they place their brush upon the paper?
I only wish I could create such beauty on a canvas. Whenever I try to create a work of art, it resembles the endeavours of a rather disturbed toddler.

Fortunately, my own ineptitude doesn't stop me from
admiring the work of others. About twelve years ago, as
I was walking around a local art exhibition I was strongly
drawn to the work of a particular artist whose pictures
seemed to call out and invite me to spend a while looking deeper into them. I stood for a while contemplating
a stunning seascape, and admired the way this artist had
used the acrylics but then had also added bits and pieces

of other materials and metallic fragments to create layers, so that what from a distance seemed like a simple snapshot of the sea, was in fact a beautiful tapestry of colour and texture that you wanted to touch and explore.

A week or so later, after a Sunday service at church, an elegant-looking older lady approached me. She smiled and said, 'I'm not sure we have met before but I believe you are familiar with my paintings.' It was the artist, Penny. I was delighted to be able to share my enthusiasm for her work and to see the humble satisfaction in her eyes. 'I am so pleased,' she said, 'because I felt that God wanted me to give you this.' She handed me the very picture I had fallen in love with. 'I felt it could be significant in some way,' Penny continued. 'It is called "Walking on Water".'

I stopped in my tracks.

My eyes examined the picture again – those metallic stars, those iridescent shimmers – it was as if there was a trail of footprints across the water. I paused again, grateful but also stunned at the remarkable relevance this had to our lives at that moment.

We had been thinking and praying about moving to lead a different church, which was a tough and slightly scary decision, and as part of that pondering I had been reading a wonderful book by John Ortberg called *If You Want to Walk on Water, You've Got to Get Out of the Boat.*[2] I knew, as I gazed upon the waters of that picture, that this profound and transformational piece of advice was aimed right at us.

[2]John Ortberg, *If You Want to Walk of Water, You've Got to Get Out of the Boat* (Grand Rapids, MI: Zondervan, 2001)

CREATED

As I sit here now with that painting in front of me, it is without a doubt one of our most precious possessions. It is significant and special because God used Penny's creation to speak to us about coming to the church that is now our home, as well as prompting the beginning of a wonderful friendship with such a talented lady. But also, as I look at that work I know that Penny's highly skilled hands painted that canvas week after week, month after month – adding to it, perfecting it and shaping it until it expressed the inspiration in her heart and the vision in her mind's eye.

Created with Love

It is one thing to be inspired by the genius of a dancer, a sculptor or a painter, but the creative expression of God is staggering. We can only begin to reflect his splendour. He imagined and his thoughts came into being. He spoke and his words brought light and life. He carefully and lovingly wove together the majesty of creation and he looked at it and said that it was good (which feels like a slightly divine understatement).

I am sure you, like me, have surveyed a range of mountains or scrutinised the petals of a flower and been in awe at the grandeur and the complexity of the natural world. God has given us the huge responsibility of caring for and protecting his creation that surrounds us. And then there's the stuff that we can't even see. When I begin to think about what is beyond our planet or deep inside the earth, my head begins to spin a little. I remember sitting at school learning about the layers of the earth and the molten rock that was glooping around beneath my feet as our planet spins around the sun at 66,600 miles per hour and feeling completely overwhelmed by it all.

Our planet is incredible. Why not grab your nearest diamond (preferably one that you own in order to avoid arrest) and consider that this stone, which is essentially common old carbon, was slowly formed and shaped in the earth's mantle, about 150 km down in the high temperatures found beneath the crust of our planet, only to be thrust nearer to the surface by violent volcanic eruptions that deposited them in rivers and volcanic remains, where we could discover and treasure them. What an extraordinary process.

Perhaps the most thought-provoking facet of all creation is that the God who brought everything about, from stars to diamonds, also lovingly crafted us in his own image. What was it like, I wonder, for him to create us, a little lower than the angels, crowning us with glory and honour and putting everything under our feet (see Heb. 2:7–8)? What pleasure did it give him to design a planet where the kaleidoscope of his creativity might work together in harmony? Was he imagining the relationship he could have with us and the stories that would be written as we came into being? Whatever was in his mind's eye, we were made primarily with love.

King David puts it this way in Psalm 139:13–15

> For you created my inmost being;
>   you knit me together in my mother's womb.

CREATED

I praise you because I am fearfully and wonderfully made;
  your works are wonderful,
  I know that full well.
My frame was not hidden from you
  when I was made in the secret place,
  when I was woven together in the depths of the earth.

It's remarkable. Like a diamond, we were created, far from the light of day, by the Ultimate Artist so that he could treasure us. He didn't make us because he was bored or lonely. It wasn't that he needed to make us or that his ego needed to be worshipped. No, we were created because God is love and he chose to lovingly create us to fulfil his eternal plan.

It might be that somebody once told you that you were a mistake or a disappointment, but that is not what the Bible says about you. The perfect Creator God lovingly made you, and he doesn't make mistakes. He thinks you are pretty special. No matter how misunderstood or taken for granted you might sometimes feel, you can decide to believe what others say about you, or what God says about you, his precious creation. You are designed and adored.

A Master Craftsman

One of the things I have discovered in recent years is how painstaking a process it is to create anything. Whether you plan to make a wooden cabinet, write a poem, design a website, compose a song or bake a fancy cake, it is always a labour of love. Certainly, the writing of this book has been a test of character, I can assure you. But none of us can produce something worthwhile or truly remarkable in an instant; it takes years of training, followed by hours of forming, tweaking, getting frustrated, yelling at the cat, working harder, drinking coffee and finally polishing our prized creation.

I have created many less than successful 'masterpieces' over the years. For example, in our house we have a unique dessert called 'splumble'. I thought any sucker could make an apple crumble – I mean, how hard could it be? I was wrong. The mixture that topped my mashed fruit could have more properly been used to render a house. My kids did try to eat their pudding, bless their hearts, politely cutting it, and then chewing it, chewing it and chewing it, until they renamed the dish so that the words 'splodge' combined with 'crumble' to fairly represent my efforts. (I have since made a secret discovery that has changed my life: canned fruit and pre-prepared bags of crumble. Don't knock it.)

A similar level of success was achieved during what my family call my 'quilting phase'. I started rather well, actually. I planned it carefully, I cut out the pieces with the precision of a surgeon. I began to construct the pieces with mind-numbing perfectionism, and then . . . to be honest, I got bored. I started to run that fabric through the sewing machine like it was on fire, bypassing the need for hassly pins or fiddly edging. Who has time for that kind of gubbins? Let's just say that there are sacks of potatoes with more finesse than my finished quilt, but I love it anyway.

I ended those projects with something far greater than the results of my culinary or stitched efforts. I gained a deep admiration for people who have the patience and the skill to accomplish something truly beautiful. I developed a genuine appreciation of the kind of temperament and discipline that it takes to lovingly craft something from its inception until its completion.

I love the way that Paul in Ephesians 2:10 (NLT) says, 'For we are God's masterpiece. He has created us anew in Christ Jesus, so that we can do the good things he planned for us long ago.' Who would not love to be described as a masterpiece? Sure, after a bad night's sleep I might look a bit more like a Picasso than a Rembrandt, but I am encouraged that I am apparently a work of art nonetheless. Just as we would never imagine Michelangelo cobbling together a work of art, neither are we randomly thrown together or casually constructed. We are shaped and sculpted by the creator of the universe with unconditional love in his heart, and we were made for him and for a purpose.

But even a masterpiece has a bad day at the office. Peter Cropper, the acclaimed violinist, was once fortunate enough to be given a 258-year-old handcrafted Stradivarius by the Royal Academy of Music for a series of concerts. It was a rare and special privilege even to be able to hold this musical work of art. But as he stepped onto the stage to the applause of his audience, Peter tripped and fell onto that rare treasure of an instrument and snapped the neck right off.

A priceless masterpiece, in one moment, destroyed.

He was inconsolable and the Royal Academy considered the violin to be beyond repair. But the violin was then placed into the hands of a master craftsman in the hope that despite the years of being played and the seemingly irreparable damage, it might possibly be restored. Somehow, that craftsman did what was thought to be impossible. Not only was the violin invisibly repaired, but as Peter Cropper continued to move his bow over the strings in the remaining concerts, it played with a sound even more resonant and exquisite than before.

Not only did God create us, but also his word tells us that when we trust in him we are 'new creations' (2 Cor. 5:17). It is as if our heavenly master craftsman recreates us and mends the mess in our hearts as he repairs our relationship with him through Christ. He longs for our lives to sing his melody in our own unique way, and he will restore and recreate us into the masterpiece he designed us to be. I love the image in Isaiah 64:8 where we are reminded, 'You, Lord, are our Father. We are the clay, you are the potter; we are all the work of your hand.' Sometimes I just sit and thank God again that his expert hands are always at work, reshaping me and repairing my fragile heart so that it will resound with more of his goodness.

Creative at the Core

Maybe you are one of those people who suspects that they don't have a creative bone in their body. Over the years, I have met many people who don't consider themselves to be creatively inclined. But let me challenge that thought. You were made in the image of Creator God, which means that you already have creative DNA in you, whether you are an instinctively artistic person or not. Just as a diamond's purpose is to reflect what it is made of, so we, too, reflect and express something of God as we join him in his

> All of us, at some level, have a longing in our souls for something more imaginative and powerful than mere existence.

creative mission and as we care for his creation. All of us, at some level, have a longing in our souls for something more imaginative and powerful than mere existence. Humans throughout history have always searched for the knowledge that we have been created, and for a way to be part of the creative process of life.

I remember sitting in church with a friend who is enormously artistically talented and watching her, with her box of pencils and her sketchpad, recreate the sermon visually. It was all there. Using only a few words and a palette of colours and shapes, she managed to capture the essence of the talk, and the flow of the thoughts. I was struck, not only by her incredible talent, but also by how simply the pages recalled the spirit and substance of different sermons, week after week. The images seemed so clear and compelling compared to my notebook, stuffed with page after page of words and bullet points.

So I decided to give it a go.

Now, nobody is going to transform the pages of my notebook into birthday cards to sell, and my biro-scribbled pictures, doodles and words are far from accomplished. But honestly, it has been a revelation! Within a moment of looking at any particular page, I can tell you the point of that talk and how I was responding to it at the time. It is as if my thoughts and impressions have been gathered and expressed in those images. It's interesting that more often than not we exclude ourselves from the freedom to be creative, because we allow our talent to be the barometer of our involvement and we are using Van Gogh as our benchmark. But creativity was never supposed to be professionalised – it is in all of us.

It's not surprising, then, that finding a creative outlet is often a great release for people. When I have had the opportunity to make cards with friends, to paint with the children or to arrange music with a band, I have witnessed the way in which people become so absorbed in the creative process that they visibly relax and find the freedom to let their thoughts and feelings flow in a way that would never happen within the rigid constraints of daily life.

I am not sure what creative endeavours you would most enjoy. If push came to shove, I would say I'm essentially a massive paintbrush and a wall kind of girl. I must have bought about 25 million house magazines over the years, none of which I could ever throw away (just in case), and choosing a paint colour for a room has been known to take me a week and enough tester pots to paint the entire Forth Bridge in various shades of cream. Post painting-frenzy, I then get genuinely excited by completing the effect with matching lamps, cushions and throws, which my long-suffering husband still doesn't seem to understand at all. But as strange as it might sound to some people, I find decorating to be a satisfying and creative process.

Other people I know love to build sheds, or design websites, or lovingly shape the perfect flowerbed in their garden. There are, for all of us, those moments of 'flow' where time gets lost, the other stresses of the day fall away into the background and our heart beats in time with our Maker as we are absorbed in the gratifying process of creation.

Artists at Work

The creative church leader and author of *The Artisan Soul*, Erwin McManus, encourages us to believe that, 'We are all artists at work and works of art.'[3] Every day we are engaged in the important and spiritual process of crafting the very fabric of our lives. Just as the finest sculptures don't just instantaneously appear but are formed as the material is worked and shaped, so each of us need to be active and intentional as we craft and mould the material of our dreams and desires.

> Every day we are engaged in the important and spiritual process of crafting the very fabric of our lives.

It takes some bravery to innovate in life. Every creative step we take is always a courageous step. If you are

[3]Erwin McManus, *The Artisan Soul: Crafting Your Life into a Work of Art* (New York: HarperCollins, 2014)

an artist, every time you pick up your paintbrush you risk misunderstanding or failure. And every one of us, as we create our lives, experiences a level of vulnerability as we struggle to express the longings of our soul. When we step out to explore a new horizon or try something new, we might not get it all right first time. We will probably even doubt our own intuition every now and then. But giving ourselves permission to give things a go and to learn through trial and inevitable error is crucial to the creative process, and will open up the potential for us to forge something truly original and significant.

Many of us have been guilty of inadvertently separating spirituality and creativity. It is true that the evidence in some of our churches would hardly suggest a riot of artistic freedom, but that has not always been the case. Many of us have admired the ornately decorated Gospels in the *Book of Kells*, or sat in the silence of a grand cathedral, or even been lost in the harmonies of Handel's *Messiah* and sensed that as we allow these exquisite devotional works of art to infuse our soul, we are sharing something of the magnificent heart of our creator with pilgrims throughout history. Thank God that so many of our churches and festivals are again equipping and releasing the various artists in our midst to reimagine a dynamic and creative community of faith through every modern medium.

Our desire to design and to shape our world is not just limited to Sundays and so-called 'sacred spaces'. Everywhere belongs to God and has the potential for us to add colour and flair. Have you ever experienced a waitress or a teacher who is giving their work their creative best efforts?

CREATED

It's a pleasure to watch them shine and innovate with the gifts God has given them. If we see ourselves as people who are intentionally creating lives of worth, our context is simply the place in which we can offer God our creativity. I think of a surgeon in our church who, after remodelling hips and crafting bone-cement during the day, renovates and remodels our church building in his spare time. I think of another friend who protects the environment through his work all week, and then creates an environment of worship through his music and songs on a Sunday. These people have been created to create; they are works of art and artists at work, wherever they are.

It has often been said that if it is really true that God 'is able to do immeasurably more than all we ask or imagine, according to his power that is at work within us' (Eph. 3:20), then perhaps it is time to ask for some more imagination. After all, God is not going to run out of ideas any time soon. He wants us to recapture and reinterpret the truth that we have been created in his image and to live a life inspired by him. The extraordinary Master Craftsman still has a story of faith, hope and love to tell, and he wants to express it through the canvas of our lives.

Imagine that.

DIGGING DEEPER

- Have you ever thought about how a diamond is created? What aspect of God's creation do you find most inspiring or mind-blowing?

- What aspect of the Psalm 139 extract impacts you the most about the way that you were created?

- Do you tend to believe what others say about you or what God says about you? How could you focus more on what God says?

- Do you consider yourself to be a creative person? In which areas do you express the most creativity? Digital, artistic, words, DIY . . .

- How could you find more space for creativity? Or perhaps you could notice the creativity in what you do? Is there a way you could more intentionally connect with God through the creative process?

- Is it possible to create the life you desire? What in our lives can we create with God's help, some vision and self-discipline?

- Is there something in your imagination you would love to create or achieve? Take some time to explore that with your creator.

Creator God,

I thank you for the abundance and beauty of your creation, and pray I would grasp the ways I can play my part in caring for the world in which you have placed me. Thank you that I am more than a genetic jigsaw, I am your child and I am fearfully and wonderfully made. Thank you that you are inviting me on a creative process, and I pray that as I shape my life with you as my guide, my imagination would be ignited and I would express the goodness of your love to me in new ways, with renewed purpose.

I ask these things so that my life may reflect a glimpse of your glory,

Amen

STRENGTH

Chapter 4

FLAWED

And the words of the Lord are flawless, like silver purified in a crucible, like gold refined seven times.

Psalm 12:6

It would be fair to say that my first engagement ring was not exactly a dazzler. When Mark and I got engaged, we were so strapped for cash that you would have needed the Hubble Space Telescope to find the diamond chip that was implanted into the gold somewhere on my fourth finger. But after about ten lacklustre years (I am talking about the ring, folks), that little chip decided it had had enough and made a jump for freedom. So there we were, ten years on and in the position where really we 'needed' to get me another ring. Happy days.

We were visiting the USA, and decided it would be a good idea to look for rings while we were there. We had budgeted for a replacement (but significantly upgraded) ring, and that was all well and good, except it turned out to be a far more intricate and complicated process than I had ever expected. Buying a diamond, it turns out, could be a full-time job (nice work if you can get it). Some might suggest, I suppose, that this rather arduous decision-making process might have been marginally exacerbated by my being a bit of a research junkie, and they would be right. It is well established amongst those who have known me for more than – oh I don't know – say five minutes, that I am, without question, the heavyweight queen of research, who likes to know everything about a subject, whether that is a potential holiday destination or a new washing machine. I exhaust myself sometimes, never mind those around me.

It turns out, though, that diamonds are a lot more exciting to research than washing machine spin speeds and their drying time ratios. Having never really looked at diamonds very closely before, we had no idea that all diamonds were classified by the four Cs – colour, cut, carats and clarity. I could understand that how white and sparkly they were (colour), what shape they were (cut) and how huge or tiny they were (carats) would affect the price, but I knew nothing about a diamond's clarity.

That all changed the moment the shop assistant gave me a microscope.

Inclusions are Normal

There they were, magnified for all to see – these tiny imperfections. Little shapes, spots or cloudy areas – each stone uniquely flawed by its own intrinsic defects. Some of these miniscule marks were made during the formation of the stone as it crystallised and others had been added through wear and tear in the ground or during the process of excavation and cutting. And the diamonds with the greatest clarity, with the fewest possible flaws, obviously command the highest value – although a flawless diamond is not exactly easy to find.

What we found particularly interesting was that these flaws or imperfections are called 'inclusions'. Like a birthmark or a fingerprint, each diamond has its completely unique little idiosyncrasies included as part of its identity. It is to be expected. It is quite acceptable.

Flawlessness is an unattainable ideal – in our jewels and, more importantly, in our character. After all, not a person alive is flawless – that privilege belonged to Jesus alone. Every one of us has our cloudy areas, weaknesses or character imperfections and, let's be honest, most of us don't need a microscope in order to identify these inclusions. Much of the time, we rather wish that these 'flaws' were far less visible to the outside world or that we could simply polish them out. If only the things we feel most insecure or most embarrassed about were only surface deep and could be buffed up and eliminated so easily! No, sadly, these inclusions are not smudges on the surface of our life – they are much deeper than that. In fact, many of our obvious inclusions are an integral part of who we are – formed either as an inevitable result of the crystallisation of our temperament or established as part of who we are during the tough process of being shaped by the knocks and bumps of life.

A Microscope Mentality

But here lies the danger.

When you and I take out our metaphorical microscopes and focus upon and magnify these inclusions, which are an intrinsic part of our distinctive and complex personality, we will drive ourselves crazy with frustration at our perceived imperfection. I have lost count of the times I have endlessly chastised myself for being too loud and excitable here or too expressive or direct there, as if I can do anything about my rather outgoing temperament.

I wonder how many times you have found yourself magnifying your own inadequacies or continually bringing them back into the focus of your thinking or conversations? I suspect, like me, you have even deflected compliments or praise to refocus people on your supposed incompetence.

'What a lovely house you have. You have great taste.'

'Oh, really? It's all done on the cheap and I have only painted half the rooms.'

'I loved your presentation today. It was so interesting and you were so confident.'

'You have to be kidding! I was so nervous I was shaking, and I had no time to prepare it properly.'

You know the kind of thing. And it is a symptom of a much deeper problem. We *know* we can't be perfect, we accept logically that people make mistakes and can't be good at everything, and yet we somehow *behave* in a way that indicates that is not what we truly believe at all.

We can be given thirty compliments about a certain performance or piece of work and one criticism, and of course what remains with us is that one criticism. It dominates our thinking and buries itself into our subconscious. We overlook being told we are funny, thoughtful, clever or generous but hold on to words like standoffish or bossy as if they were labels that cannot ever be removed. Some of these words have stuck to us for decades, like toxic sticky bandages that limit our movement and shape our identity.

Of course, there is always a need to become more self-aware and to be appropriate to our circumstances but, to my knowledge, personality transplants are still unavailable on the NHS. So why would I stare continually at these perceived inadequacies, scrutinising and reclassifying myself as significantly flawed as a result of who I am?

Why indeed.

Perfectionism is a Chore

Day by day, perfectly sane people beat themselves up as they stare down their microscope at the things that make them feel inferior or messed up. Some of us become far too perfectionist for our own good, especially if for various reasons we do not feel acceptable in some way. We embark on a subconscious quest to eliminate any sign of weakness in a vain attempt to show the world and ourselves that we are really doing okay and are in control of our lives. After all, it's nice to kid yourself that you're in charge.

But rather like vacuuming and dusting, perfectionism is a chore that is never finished. It constantly whispers at you, 'Couldn't you work just a bit harder on this?' 'Couldn't you try to make her a little bit happier?' 'Couldn't that piece of work be slightly better?' 'Wouldn't your boots be marginally more fabulous if they were exactly the right height for your jeans?' (Okay, the boots are less significant, but you'd be amazed . . .)

> Rather like vacuuming and dusting, perfectionism is a chore that is never finished.

We even fuel this miserable quest for flawlessness by observing the fabulousness of other people and their careers, houses, outfits and families. Goodness me, other people's children look so happy on social media. In fact, judging by my newsfeed, it seems to me that everybody I know is either merrily jogging or sitting contentedly on a beach. Away from the computer, I need an intravenous chocolate infusion to even contemplate picking up the average magazine which so helpfully instructs me about how to be skinny, cook brilliantly, run a fabulous business from the spare room and be a flexible and sexy kind of Swiss-army-wife.

Give me a break.

The apostle Paul missed social media and women's mags by a few centuries, but he knew that we tend to make judgements about each other and ourselves, even within our church community. Writing to the New Testament church, he reminds them (and therefore us) to get a grip (my translation) and remember that we each have a valuable and vital role to play:

> If the whole body were an eye, where would the sense of hearing be? If the whole body were an ear, where would the sense of smell be? But in fact God has placed the parts in the body, every one of them, just as he wanted them to be. If they were all one part, where would the body be?
>
> 1 Corinthians 12:17–19

Paul was definitely scratching an itch we still feel today. We might turn up at church or work and admire the gifts and strengths of others and then begin to weigh up our own lack of confidence or effectiveness in that area in response. In our minds, as we elevate them, we subtly diminish or degrade our own worth or value. We see the trendy worship leader with his flicky hair, we listen to his raspy voice as he plays the guitar and joins the angels in worship, and we feel that perhaps our ministry in serving coffee and tea with a few digestives isn't quite so awe-inspiring after all. But what if, in all reality, the most significant conversation and the most God-inhabited moment of the whole morning was to be found as somebody welcomed a struggling single parent with a warm cup of tea and a comfy chair, listening to them with compassion and speaking words of hope into their life? A worship leader is a servant of God, using his or her gifts and talents in a vulnerable and public ministry, but the gift of hospitality is no less worthy or significant.

Reversed Strengths

One of the glorious things about life is that my deficiencies are somebody else's greatest passion. How good is that?! Similarly, I have discovered, to my amazement, that the things I think are of utmost importance don't seem to bother somebody else at all. That doesn't make me right or them wrong, although sometimes I admit I think so; it just

We are all flawed but fabulous, in different ways.

reinforces the fact that God has got all the bases covered as he puts his team together, and that we need to grow in our understanding and appreciation of each other. We are all flawed but fabulous, in different ways. We all have our areas of natural or developed strength, and other areas where things don't come so easily to us.

How liberating to discover, then, that many of the things we struggle with or perceive to be our flaws are simply the reverse side of our biggest strengths. They are inevitable inclusions due to the way we have been formed and shaped. For example, you might be a brilliant listener and somebody who is deeply empathetic, but you might then also find it difficult to speak assertively about your own needs or to speak to more than one person at a time. Same personality; different perspective. Or maybe you are somebody who loves to organise and leads confidently, but you might also find it hard to let others contribute or to wait patiently while others make decisions more slowly. Or how about you wonderfully creative people who are passionate, expressive and emotional, but who find it hard to keep your house tidy or your administration under control? It is surprising how often our biggest strength can be so closely linked to our biggest struggle.

I remember my husband Mark being interviewed for a particular post after he left Bible College. Being Baptists, we like to make prospective ministers and their wives go through the most gruelling process possible, and so we spent a few days with the potential new church, where Mark and I smiled until our faces ached and Mark spoke at various meetings, after which they took a vote to decide whether he was suitable. I know, it's a real blast. When the church called Mark a week later to inform him that he had not got the job, it took him a while to uncover the reason behind the rejection. It seemed strange – he had received such a warm reception and felt he had delivered his presentations well. Eventually, the person on the other end of the phone relented and told him that I, as his wife, was probably not entirely suitable. I talked too much and I laughed too loudly, and they felt this meant I probably had issues that might reflect badly on Mark going into ministry.

It was not a happy day.

But while I accept I probably did chat non-stop, and I do have an undeniably raucous laugh, what struck me was that as I was (apparently) not being interviewed – they'd had no opportunity to discover what my personality actually enables me to do. Had they asked, they would have seen that the flipside of what they felt to be my flawed extroversion was that at the ripe old age of 23, I had already preached in dozens of churches, performed and sung at numerous events, had run various children's holiday clubs and family services, had a degree in PR and had been a professional fundraiser.

Needless to say, God had good plans in store for us in another church, where both Mark and I flourished and learned to grow in our gifts as well as navigating our numerous weaknesses.

We can find great freedom in acknowledging and accepting that it's okay to not be flawless – mistakes and failure are an inevitable result of getting out of bed in the morning or trying anything new. And some things will always be a natural and intrinsic result of who we are, and could even be a reflection of a particular strength that we have. When we can identify these related traits, our mission should be to invest significantly more time and attention in building our strengths than trying to constantly circumnavigate our weaknesses. It is a powerful and far healthier paradigm for us to adjust our focus from being defined by 'what we are not' and 'what we can not', to realising instead that we are the proud owners of 'what we are' and 'what we can'.

A Realistic Assessment

Almost every attitude we express or deliberate action we take begins with a silent conversation in our minds. So much of what we experience is because of what we think. Sometimes we say downright unpleasant things about ourselves to ourselves that we would never allow anybody else to say about us. We really should think more about what we think. One moment we swallow a generous dose of self-righteousness and pride, and the next we chug down a mighty measure of self-loathing or bitterness. Then we add into the mix the memories of toxic words and opinions of others, and before we know it our thoughts can poison our potential.

Somehow we have to break free from this unhelpful internal conversation. So where do we find the antidote to this thinking? Paul in Romans 12:2–3 tells us this:

> Do not conform to the pattern of this world, but be transformed by the renewing of your mind. Then you will be able to test and approve what God's will is – his good, pleasing and perfect will. For by the grace given me I say to every one of you: do not think of yourself more highly than you ought, but rather think of yourself with sober judgement, in accordance with the faith God has distributed to each of you.

A sober, honest and reasonable assessment of our character is a precious gift we can all give to ourselves. We are neither the most brilliant, intelligent and beautiful person that ever walked the planet, but nor are we the dullest, the slowest or the ugliest. That's normal. So let's challenge our own thinking.

In fact, these verses tell us that God has distributed enough faith to us to realign our thoughts around how he sees us. It's important that we do deploy our faith when reflecting upon how we see ourselves, because we need God at the centre of that conversation in order to renew our mind. He has given us everything we need to drag ourselves out of any pools of self-pity or discontent where we have made ourselves a little bit too comfortable. Maybe you, like me, have spent some really good hippo-time over the years, languishing in the muddy feelings of inadequacy or wallowing in rejection, but the problem is that the longer we stay in those pools, the harder they are to get out of.

Engaging our faith will also guard us against the kind of over-confidence that can equally obscure the reality of our own flaws and limitations. Have you ever cringed at the participants on TV shows like *The Apprentice*, who seem to have more confidence than is warranted given their ability? None of us want to be that person. And many of us will have experienced ambitious colleagues who seem to have no awareness of their lack of suitability or experience for the promotion they are chasing. It's not a good trait.

No wonder Paul tells us to be transformed by the renewing of our minds. As we get our thinking straightened out, much of our life will straighten out as a result.

As we get our thinking straightened out, much of our life will straighten out as a result.

This is why we need to constantly choose to put the flawless and refined word of God (Psalm 12:6) front and centre in our view. As we immerse ourselves in scripture and the truths of God as well as the truths about us, we will be able to test and approve what God's will is for our lives, giving us the kind of wisdom and clarity that we long for.

A Telescope Tendency

But here is something I find very interesting. While we tend to zoom in to and magnify the areas of ourselves that make us feel deficient or embarrassed, in a rather perverse and self-serving way we show an almost reverse strategy in our approach to the flaws and blemishes in our lives that we could and should actually do something about. We rather conveniently ditch the microscope and pick up the wrong end of a telescope to zoom out, looking far, far away at the mistakes, stupid words, pride and plain old sin which, in truth, could do with a bit more close-up analysis.

It is, of course, part of our human nature that we will get it right some of the time, and get it spectacularly wrong on other occasions. We will be motivated by love on one day and behave selfishly another. That doesn't make us unblemished today and an abject failure tomorrow. But neither should this lead us to simply shrug our shoulders and say, 'Oh well, nobody's perfect.' Being realistic is not the same as being resigned.

But make no mistake, our propensity for looking down a reversed telescope and explaining away our less than model behaviour is boundless. We will do whatever it takes to convince others and ourselves that we really are good and respectable, even if it means twisting our motives around in our minds. It is amazing how, with some mental gymnastics, a bit of gossip can mystically morph into sharing a pastoral concern, and surely we can justify a teensy (huge) bit of self-indulgence after working so very hard, never mind whether we can afford it or whether it is advisable.

But the trouble with avoidance is that you can't avoid things forever, and things are almost always easier to deal with, the earlier we deal with them. If we choose to look away from our hearts for too long, we may well become immune to the nudges of the Holy Spirit as he prompts us to address these flaws that are not intended to be a part of our identity in Christ. And this unintentional neglect of our souls may well eventually obscure our vision and lead us away from the path of purity and holiness that God sees as such a priority in our lives.

What a relief that our Heavenly Father knows us more intimately and completely than we sometimes remember. He can see every bubble, cut and dark carbon spot in our hearts, but has lovingly and unconditionally committed himself to shaping us and restoring us anyway. He knows the pain we have experienced, and the things that we are ashamed of that nobody else is aware of. He knows our blind spots, and how we distract other people and even ourselves from the things that cause us most discomfort. He knows every thing we wish we had never done (sins of commission) and all of the things we really should have done but didn't (sins of omission). Our patient Heavenly Father knows more about us than we will ever realise but loves us anyway.

Clarity of Vision

While God sees all things with 20/20 vision, the human eye can only see so much. When we gaze into a diamond to gauge its clarity based on the flaws and blemishes hidden within, we will need the help of an expert and a strong microscope. Likewise, we need the Holy Spirit to enhance our inner vision as we ask each day for help with what we can see and all that is beyond our view.

Whether it is in a diamond or whether it is the ability to discern the path ahead with confidence, clarity is something that we always value. There is no doubt that our vision will be greatly improved as we both remove the microscope's magnification from things we should not be scrutinising and equally refuse to banish to a galaxy far, far away the things that really do require some more attention. We need to focus on the right stuff and loosen our grip on the rest.

But added to that, we might also want to look again at the areas where we have struggled the most to see if that might be the very flaw or challenge that God can, in fact, use the most. If we have overcome an addiction, we have something powerful to say to those who are still trapped where we were. If we have lost our temper as a parent, we can come alongside the exhausted mother with genuine empathy. Where we have been shown mercy, we have mercy to share.

We are not flawless, but we are new creations. We are imperfect people in an imperfect world, but we have a perfect God and his flawless words as our guide. Sure, we might be a bit bruised, we might have our issues and we struggle with stuff, just like everybody else. But let's not forget that we have our strengths, our experiences and our opportunities to share too, and God wants to use them all for his glory.

DIGGING DEEPER

- Have you ever looked at a diamond under a microscope? How did the inclusions appear to you?

- Can you recall specific occasions where you have magnified or drawn attention to your flaws?

- To what extent would you say you suffer from perfectionism or comparing yourself with others? Does this ever change?

- Can you identify the reverse sides of a strength and weakness that you have?

- How could you build on your strengths instead of focusing on your weaknesses?

- How could you allow your mind to be renewed by the word of God?

- When are you most aware of God speaking to you about the things you have got wrong?

- What areas of your life where you have struggled could God use to encourage, comfort or train others?

Heavenly Father,

Once again, I thank you that although I may be flawed, I am loved unconditionally by you. I thank you for the life, the sacrificial death and the resurrection of your perfect Son, Jesus, and pray that I would see both my success and failure through your eyes. Forgive me for the times I have let you down. Use both my strengths and my struggles to bring glory to you and blessing to others.

In the powerful and flawless name of Jesus,

Amen

Chapter 5

CONNECTED

My command is this: love each other as I have loved you. Greater love has no one than this: to lay down one's life for one's friends.

John 15:12–13

I've had some strange jobs in my time. But perhaps the oddest of all was invigilating exams for cadets in the merchant navy. I would stand, sit and walk up and down for hours in silence (a substantial achievement for me – ask anyone) while the students in their smart uniforms completed page after page of engineering equations or celestial navigation charts. In order to prevent myself going absolutely bonkers and breaking into spontaneous songs from the musicals, I would find myself doing all kinds of things: memorising poems, making animals out of Blu-Tack (you'd be surprised) and eventually taking in every microscopic detail of the maps and posters on the walls. Most of them were not particularly inspiring, but there was one poster in one room that always caught my attention and I would return to read it again and again. It explained in detail the chemistry of a diamond.

Diamond has, so the poster informs me, an isometric crystallography. I know, right. So basically, the crystal structure of a diamond, called a face-centred cubic lattice, is a result of the way each carbon atom joins four other carbon atoms in regular tetrahedrons or triangular prisms. The point of this mind-bending science is this: the unique carbon structure of a diamond gives it a strength that its carbon relatives such as graphite could only dream of. And the significant difference is the way in which each atom is bonded to four other atoms. Those connections are the crucial reason why diamonds are so strong.

Divine Connections

At the very start of the Bible in Genesis 1, God intentionally forms the natural order of the world and designs us to be connected to our surroundings. God is love. His creation is an expression of his love and desire for relationship. He is the source of every good thing, and we are made, firstly and foremostly, to walk intimately with him. Our connection with our Creator and Father is at the core of our strength. But it's important to note that we are also inextricably linked to the rest of creation, of which we are a part. Our connection with creation, our food chain, our environment and how we work is vital: by the way we live we can either help sustain or we can endlessly deplete what God has given us to steward. But God gave us more still. He blessed us with the opportunity to relate with others. We were not created to be isolated or alone. We are formed for life-giving human relationships.

We are divinely connected. You and I have been woven into the tapestry of creation, and we are bonded to God, our world and each other. And those bonds, when they are strong, make us stronger too.

> You and I have been woven into the tapestry of creation, and we are bonded to God, our world and each other.

Several years ago, I was part of a small group in our church that reminded me of the strength found in being connected to others. We might not have known each other well when we first started to meet, but week in, week out, as we began to share our diverse lives and seek together the wisdom of God, we grew firm in our friendship. As our little tribe grew in strength, we held each other up through times of marriage turmoil, bouts of anger, job interviews, parental angst and extreme tiredness. And we also laughed and ate together, and rejoiced over every breakthrough, birthday and answer to prayer. There were many weeks, after a long day, when I felt almost too tired or busy to make those meetings a priority, but I am so glad I did. The bonds that we formed in that season made life richer and us all stronger.

It is impossible to flourish alone. Instead, in an ideal world, we would all enjoy friends who make us laugh and listen to us cry, a family with whom we can share the developing chapters of our life, and mentors and colleagues who make a deeply significant investment in our growth and with whom we share a meaningful purpose.

Digging for DIAMONDS

It's a shame that we can't buy this range of relationships from e-bay; not many of us feel we are as strongly connected as we would like to be, after all. But most of us have a handful of people who 'get us' and with whom we share a deep connection. What if we were to really stop and notice those divine connections that God has already given us and really value them? Could we perhaps invest more into those precious relationships and protect them more intentionally?

About a year ago, some friends loaned Mark and I the box set of the series *West Wing*.[4] I will be honest, I did not think I had time in my life for seven series of anything, but we became quickly addicted. In fact, after 117 hours, when it eventually finished, we wondered if there would be anything left in our marriage to talk about. The series, following the fictional President of the United States of America and his team in the West Wing took us through the highs of elections and the lows of international crises. We saw their relationships challenged, their friendships grow and their loyalty tested. At one point, the White House Communications Director Toby Ziegler summed up in words the strength of their incredible connection: 'We're a group. We're a team. From the President and Leo on through, we're a team. We win together, we lose together, we celebrate and we mourn together. And defeats are softened and victories sweetened because we did them together.'

All of us grow stronger when we are connected to each other. God may not have given us every relationship we

[4]Aaron Sorkin, *West Wing* (USA: Warner Bros Television, 1999)

have longed for, and not every person makes us stronger (that's for sure), but we can be deliberately thankful for those with whom we are meaningfully bonded, and continue to build other strong and life-giving connections.

Opaque Fatigue

It's an increasingly superficial world out there, but underneath it all we still long for deep and genuine relationships. We all want to interact with people who are transparent and real; who invite us into their inner world and say, 'This is me. My hopes. My fears. My desires. Let's do life together.' But we have to play our part too. Have you ever been guilty of demanding a high level of transparency from others while remaining opaque yourself? It's an easy thing to do. But it is the mutual vulnerability that comes with sharing our weaknesses and our dreams together that builds a deeper relationship and a long-lasting bond of trust.

We are, though, all very different. Have you ever wondered what happens when an extrovert meets an introvert? They get married and drive each other crazy. Let's take that further. What happens when you take a collection of people from every age and background, with a shared faith but little else in common and put them together? They get called a church and live with their leaders happily ever after.

Maybe.

Although we long for a Spirit-filled community of trust, transparency and deep connections, the potential for tension or disconnection is always there in such an unlikely tribe of disciples. But nevertheless, we are called to love God and each other, and not in a superficial way. John 13:34–35 says, 'A new command I give you: love one another. As I have loved you, so you must love one another.

By this everyone will know that you are my disciples, if you love one another.' Our goal is to love each other so deeply that it provokes a response in people. The family of God is called to practise self-giving, self-sacrificing love – in our friendships, in our marriages, in our mentoring, in our small groups, in our serving. It's certainly not easy to love as God loves us – hurt people hurt people, after all. But forgiven people must also forgive people, and somehow we must move beyond the snares of suspicion and superficiality into redeemed relationships of hope that speak of Jesus living in us.

The Transparency Trap

Transparency, however, is not the same as unfiltered outspokenness. The only people who ever get away with that kind of behaviour are young children. They have no shame. Spend more than a few minutes with your average threenager and they will tell you exactly what they want, and when they want it, without worrying about who they offend.

I remember when my daughter Isabelle was 4 years old and I made the mistake of taking her supermarket shopping. I had successfully managed to navigate the vegetables without too much drama but as I passed the clothing section she became increasingly animated, pointing and tugging at my jacket. I looked over and saw the object of her desire: a Princess Jasmine dressing up outfit. I tried to explain to her totally irrational preschool brain that the outfit was staying in the shop, but she was not to be persuaded. Within a minute Isabelle was having a full-scale meltdown in the middle of the aisle. After a few moments of panic, I picked her up and wrestled her body under my arm to leave, but in the midst of the squirming and screaming, she managed to bring down a display of wine bottles to the floor.

She sobbed. I sobbed. And as I walked the walk of shame from that store, serenaded by the tutting of tongues and the rolling of eyes, I swore that if I was ever Prime Minister, Disney princesses would be banished into the abyss forever.

Ten years later, my now teenage daughter had to dress up for a night at a summer festival. What did she choose as her outfit? Princess Jasmine. You have to give her credit for knowing what she wants.

I have met a few adult children in my time too. Grown men and women who employ the same tactics as their tiny gurus, saying whatever they think and sulking or throwing a tantrum if their wishes are not fulfilled. You'll find them saying things like, 'Well, I'm just being honest, so I am going to tell you it as it is,' or 'I liked that service as it was. Give me back my service or I am leaving.' Perhaps their mothers never taught them to calm down and eat their broccoli.

But by the time we have left reception year, most of us have learnt that being indiscriminately honest can land you in a whole load of trouble. Honesty is not supposed to be a weapon from which others need protection. You and I do not always have the right to be right or to candidly express every opinion and resentment that we own.

However, we are called again and again to love.

A Safe Place

David, as a shepherd and a king, knew that the place for his most raw and unedited emotion was before God. In the Psalms we witness him pouring out his anguish, his insecurity and his doubts. Like David, being deeply connected to a God who accepts us warts and all, enables us to sift our thoughts and feelings in a completely safe place so we can live, love and lead others with his wisdom, truth and love as our source.

It also enables us to create a safe place for each other. Not to rant, gossip or constantly offload, but to share a secure space of compassion and growth. As a rule, we will share what we feel safe to share, and a trusted friend, spouse or mentor who will work through our deepest thinking with us, helping us to grow stronger is a rare treasure that will make our soul richer. As we value this in others, so we can also play our part in making it safe for others to share with us. Did you realise that your home, your office, in fact your very presence can be a place where others can come, knowing they are loved and valued? We can create an atmosphere of acceptance and kindness, as well as a place of truth and challenge. According to the book of Proverbs, what we say and how we say it can be the difference between life and death. If this is true, then we have the opportunity to engage in critical conversations every day that could be defining moments of encouragement to those around us.

Jesus is the perfect example to us in this (and every) respect. In the Gospels, he is always intentionally interested in people's lives, purposefully asking insightful questions and listening to the hopes and fears beneath the actions and the words presented to him. What a great role model. As a person who loves to talk, learning to listen is a skill that has taken a while for me to get to grips with. Some might say it's still a work in progress. The funny thing is, the more we listen, the more we learn and the better chance we have of responding in a way that brings life in all its fullness.

Quality versus Quantity

I sometimes wonder what Jesus would have done with social media. After all, he didn't try to be intimate friends with everybody, although his capacity for love was infinite. He didn't have the technology to maintain a relationship with each and every person he met or to build a platform for his ministry – although I suppose he did borrow the odd boat from time to time. What would his updates look like anyway?

> Multiplied enough food today for 5,000 people. Bit sick of tuna sandwiches now TBH. LOL!

or maybe

> @PetertheFisher gave it his best shot today walking on water. #proudofyou #stepsoffaith #shameaboutthesinkingpart

We'll never know.

Digging for DIAMONDS

Personally, I thank God for the benefits of email, texts and social media and the way that it enables a certain level of interaction with people I care about, but even with technology surrounding us all day, there are only so many strong bonds we can form in our lives. If we have 300 friends on Facebook, they can't all be intimate friends.

While we interact online, we face the constant temptation to either write thoughtlessly without engaging our brain-filters first or conversely to carefully insta-upgrade our life so that the glossy vision that we project is idealistic at best, and unbalanced at worst. Heck, with enough filters, even my cakes look delicious, and a 1970s sepia tone can make my complexion just peachy. The really strange thing is that we compare the reality of our own messy lives with the glamorous posts of others, even though we know that they are showing their edited highlights and are applying the same filters that we do! There's a whole new world of Internet-etiquette out there. My daughter told me this week that if a friend didn't have ten 'likes' on a photo in an hour, then she would remove it as it was clearly not good enough. Let's pause right there. Is this really how our friends will know that we like them?

Being able to maintain contact with friends and family all over the globe is a great thing. Connecting with charities and campaigns immediately and regularly is excellent. Being able to digest a large quantity of information and personal updates is often helpful. But, despite all of these benefits, the diet of data flowing from our digital umbilical cords can only give us so much nourishment. Quality relationships and strong bonds are only formed over time, as we touch, smile and Real love is messy and risky and trusts that people will love the real us as much as the virtual us.

share experiences together. We only really know we are loved when we know we are loved completely. It's easy to love the nice aspects of somebody or to interact with their online profile; you don't need to be Mother Teresa to do that. Real love is messy and risky and trusts that people will love the real us as much as the virtual us, through thick and thin and without the option of a de-friend button.

Thank God for the sheer quantity of connections we can now sustain. But thank him more for the quality relationships that make us stronger.

People Under Pressure

Even with our modern channels of communication and our genuine desire for strong relationships, we live in a society where the odds of forming these life-affirming bonds are increasingly stacked against us.

Over the last quarter of a century, the number of hours we spend physically and socially interacting with people has dramatically decreased. In 1971, only 17 per cent of people in the UK lived in a one-person household, whereas in 2013 that had risen to 29 per cent – that's 7.7 million people. Of those (according to research carried out by the Office of National Statistics), as many as 63 per cent admitted to feeling lonely some or all of the time, particularly if they were disabled, in poor health or widowed. In other research carried out by Relate and Relationships Scotland in 2014, a significant 42 per cent of participants said they did not consider any of their colleagues at work to be friends. But perhaps the most startling statistic of all was that one in ten people confessed to not having a single close friend.

The sad reality is that it is possible to be surrounded by people but still feel alone. We can be engaged every day in interaction that is predominantly transactional in nature. We negotiate in our workplace, we organise our dentist appointment, take part in a parent/teacher meeting or pay our bills at a bank. But these boundaried interactions, as important as they are, are limited in their potential and can often carry high levels of stress, powerplay and manipulation. Even supposedly friendly arenas of interaction can, on a bad day, feel almost gladiatorial in nature. Anybody who is a parent and has ever spent a week negotiating the school playground with other parents knows exactly what I am talking about. Lurking beneath the floral bags and baby paraphernalia lies a minefield of subtle affiliations and tribal alliances. I am convinced a whole anthropology degree could be devoted to the average school playground. But wherever we are, it is perfectly possible to be in the same space as other people, we can even be married to them, without those daily conversations ever being converted into the depth of relationship our soul longs for.

As the pace of our life continues to accelerate, so our capacity to love continues to diminish.

Perhaps one of the biggest barriers to meaningful connection with others is a lack of time. You really can't love anybody in a hurry. As the pace of our life continues to accelerate, so our capacity to love continues to diminish. We all know, in theory at least, that even the strongest relationships are unable to maintain themselves without lashings of time and effort.

I had a particularly busy day recently, which was part of a hectic week in a chaotic month. In the midst of a work deadline, balancing teenage taxi services and an evening meeting, I knew I had to bomb to the supermarket for supplies. I raced around the store, threw the bags into the boot and promptly reversed into a stationary row of trollies that had been left out of the trolley bay, breaking a rear light in the process. After running back into the store to talk in a not especially calm manner to a manager wielding endless forms, I then arrived back home fizzing with frustration, where I wrote some brief emails, cremated dinner, scrubbed the stupid burnt pans and then snapped at my children.

What a shambles.

Is it possible that as we are constantly propelled forwards on a treadmill of activity, we subconsciously make the people around us secondary to the important tasks we keep at the front of our minds? Might those closest to us sometimes end up with the leftovers of our energy, as we are too preoccupied or drained to love them in the way that they or we really want? As I've often heard said, 'The days are long but the years are short.' Time passes all too quickly. If we do not hit the pause button and find a way to connect deeply, we may find that we unintentionally let that which we treasure most highly slip through our fingers.

Digging for DIAMONDS

Let's ask ourselves whether we need to treat the 'hurry sickness' in our lives. If you think you could do with a prescription, here it is: deliberately choose the slow lane on the motorway, make way for somebody in the queue, or (gulp) strike a line through some diary entries. And make a date with somebody you love.

Rush less.

Love more.

DIGGING DEEPER

- Were you aware that a diamond is unique and strong due to its atomic construction?

- What difference does it make to you knowing, as Genesis suggests, that you are designed to be connected to God, the natural world and other people?

- Can you think of three people with whom you have connected on a particularly deep level? Are they family or friends?

- What are the biggest obstacles for you in forming close bonds with people?

- How do we encourage transparency and avoid superficiality in our relationships?

- Have you ever encountered people who are too honest? If so, how do you respond?

- How can we constructively deal with differences and conflict in our churches? Is it possible for us to be an example of community to others?

- How can you become more of a safe space for people? At work? At home?

- What can you do to make your online interactions positive and helpful? Is there anything you would change?

- What one thing can you do to develop quality relationships or strong bonds in the days ahead?

Heavenly Father,

I thank you that you are a God of love. I thank you that you want to know me and you want me to know you and others. I thank you that I am connected to all you have made and that you made me with a desire to love and be loved. I ask that I will forgive as I have been forgiven, and that I will learn more about loving you and others every day. I need your grace and your patience, Lord, and I ask for more of your power to build strong bonds that will give glory to you.

In the name of Jesus, who shows me how to love without measure,

Amen

Chapter 6

RESILIENT

We have this hope as an anchor for the soul, firm and secure.

Hebrews 6:19

A few years ago, my husband Mark and I were given a golden opportunity. We were invited to attend a small conference with a few leaders from different countries at a huge church in Chicago called Willow Creek Community Church. We were super excited. Willow Creek, and their senior leader Bill Hybels, had given us years of inspiration, and we were going to spend some time listening and learning with him and his senior staff team.

So, we arranged childcare, bought tickets and set off. The thing is, being wintertime, the windy city was now the rather snowy city. In fact, on the final day of the conference, when we were due to spend the day with Bill Hybels himself, we woke up to witness one of the worst freak snow storms that Chicago had seen for years. These people know how to do snow. They are geared up for the white stuff. But this was an uber-storm. More than a foot had fallen in the couple of hours before dawn and it was still falling in bucketloads. The government had closed the airport, the school buses were cancelled and the whole city was hidden indoors.

The whole city, that was, apart from us.

We had not crossed the world and left our children at home to miss this day. No way, José! We were going.

So, we wrapped up, went out to what was once the driveway, eventually identified which icy lump was our cheap little tin-can of a rental car, scraped the glass clear, prised the door open and started to drive. We slowly shimmied and slid down the street to the main road – slightly hampered by the fact that by the time the wipers had got to one side of the screen the rest had been completely re-covered – and eventually found a track in the middle of the road where other crazy people had been. It was, however, impossible to turn left or right out of this track, unless you wanted to join the graveyard of giant 4x4 jeeps that had been abandoned at the side of the road, having deviated from their position.

After a while, having unsuccessfully attempted a right turn in the centre of a crossroads, we temporarily got stuck and I finally burst into tears. I took a deep breath. And then I realised that there really was only one option available: to keep my eyes on the road and to keep driving.

Eventually, after what seemed like forever, we got to the church. They had deployed their divine fleet of snow-ploughs and parted the White Sea of snow in order for us to pass through to the promised car park. And verily they did say unto us, 'Well done good and faithful servants. Behold, there is a heavenly banquet of bagels and coffee waiting for you.' And we did partake in that banquet, I can assure you.

It turned out to be a truly inspiring day, and one that shaped our ministry and us in many significant ways. Thank God that somehow we kept our eyes on the road and kept driving.

The Stress Factor

It gets like that sometimes, doesn't it? We have all had those seasons where our journey of faith feels like a road that is too hard to travel. There are those times when our view of God seems obscured, the road ahead seems treacherous, the church we are travelling in seems clapped-out and our destination has become unclear.

> We have all had those seasons where our journey of faith feels like a road that is too hard to travel.

And sometimes our circumstances feel like a blizzard that doesn't know when to stop. Let's be honest, most of us have endured times when our relationships are hard, our health is a battle, our work seems like a series of challenges and our kids drive us ever so slightly crazy. And sometimes that's just a Monday! Life can be hard.

So how do we respond to this kind of pressure? How do we develop some spiritual and emotional muscle so that when the tough times come, we have some inner strength in order to cope?

Digging for DIAMONDS

Maybe the diamond can help us here. A diamond is basically a piece of coal that has handled stress remarkably well. They are both versions of carbon, but unlike coal, diamonds are supremely resilient and resistant to pressure – in fact they only exist because of pressure. They are formed into an almost indestructible material by being subjected to the incredible force of the pressure deep in the earth's mantle over a long period of time. That pressure, along with intense heat, creates a substance that is the hardest natural material on earth, topping the Mohs hardness scale at 10. Do you know what other substance is hard enough to cut a diamond? Another diamond. Even the word diamond comes from the Greek word *adamas*, meaning 'unconquerable'.

They're tough little beauties.

But they would still be coal without the pressure.

Resilience is not something we develop by reading a book about it or discussing it over dinner. Some things are only learned in the classroom of life. In the same way that courage and forgiveness only move from being concepts into reality when they are put into practice, resilience and strength of character are developed as they are deployed. All muscles, I am told, are only able to carry the weight they are designed to bear as they are used regularly.

While nobody can endure intolerable stress and pressure for indefinite amounts of time, a level of stress or pressure can actually enhance our experience of life. Stress can make us excited and alert, it can enhance our focus and creativity, and it can even teach us how to depend upon others. Pressure clarifies our priorities and reveals our character in a way that we don't always notice in easier times.

Bounce-back-ability

But whether the pressure we experience is a normal part of the rigour of everyday life or is more excessive in force, it is resilience that keeps us going. Resilience is defined as the ability to spring back into shape. It is the mental toughness that enables us to retain perspective and overcome difficulties and setbacks; to somehow not deviate from the road or to give up and go home but to keep on driving.

Our foundational years make a massive difference to how we approach setbacks and circumstances. Educationalists and psychologists tells us that many things contribute to how well our resilience muscles develop, including the level of security we have experienced, whether key transitions went well or caused us distress, whether our peers were resilient, whether the adults surrounding us gave us support and strategies to keep moving forwards, and whether we developed confidence as we achieved goals which would motivate us further.

Which makes me wonder – as parents, mentors and friends, how seriously do we take the challenge to encourage each other to be more resilient? Do we bail our children out or blame their teacher when their homework is hard? Or do we give them strategies to help them to work through it? If we

> How seriously do we take the challenge to encourage each other to be more resilient?

don't get the part in the team that we tried out for, do we sulk and feel personally rejected? Or do we accept that there are only so many places and take part in other ways? How about when our friend doesn't get the new job or the promotion at work that they worked so hard for? Do we agree that they should give up on their goals or do we encourage them to get feedback, learn from it and keep going?

It has been fascinating to see, over our years of church leadership and friendships, how different people respond to different levels of stress. Of course, some of this is personality and our natural propensity to worry, but some people really do seem to have stronger resilience muscles than others.

There are a few folk who seem to be firmly stuck in their misery, giving Eeyore a run for his money and asking, 'Why me, Lord?' at every turn of events. Nothing is less appealing than a person who is permanently engulfed in the unfairness of the world. But neither is it a blessing when we meet those ever so slightly smug chaps who have never had to wake up forty-three times in a night for a baby, had to cope with a serious illness or fought to get a house. Their lack of awareness and empathy can be astonishing. Sadly they are also the ones who sometimes come to us with fear and disappointment in their eyes when they face a bad patch in their marriage or don't get a promotion at work. It is as if they cannot believe that discomfort and struggle would be a part of their story.

The people who inspire me most are those who have had to build up their resilience muscles through grief, health challenges or redundancy, for example, and who have grown stronger through it, gaining wisdom, perspective on other smaller crises, and a compassion for others who are still struggling on the journey. They might still have their own battles to fight, but they know how to try and fight them.

Be Prepared

So how do we develop the mental toughness that life sometimes requires of us? As none of us know what our future holds (thank God) it's probably not possible to be prepared for every circumstance. After all, you could attend triple the usual antenatal classes, but nothing fully prepares anybody for labour, sleepless nights and those mysterious baby cries that send shivers down your spine. But that said, in order to strengthen ourselves spiritually and emotionally for the road ahead, we can take on board this one important principle: never confuse life with God. Life will disappoint us, and people may well break our hearts. We will, in all probability, let ourselves down too. Let's be honest about these things and accept that although life is horrible sometimes, that doesn't mean God is. Otherwise, we are liable to have a faith failure at every hurdle.

Resilience is, in essence, following Jesus and learning to apply our faith and to reach out to God in the midst of our challenges and disappointments, when we need him more than ever. We are not better Christians or more decent people if we project a veneer of shiny, polished perfection, all self-sufficient and without doubts or

We build up our endurance and resilience as we are honest with each other about our doubts and the realities of living out our faith in the difficult times.

struggles – one glimpse at the Gospels and the disciples lurching from one awkward moment to another should reassure us about that. We build up our endurance and resilience as we are honest with each other about our doubts and the realities of living out our faith in the difficult times.

No wonder God in his word spends so much time reassuring his people with words like, 'Have I not commanded you? Be strong and courageous. Do not be afraid; do not be discouraged, for the Lord your God will be with you wherever you go' (Josh. 1:9).

We will all feel out of our depth at times and need to be told these things repeatedly; there will be days when our courage will buckle, we will get discouraged and we will be filled with fear! God knows that. But rather than politely asking or suggesting that we employ whatever strength we have, he actually commands us to do it. We can, it seems, choose to build up our resilience muscles – to deliberately discern what we can still do, to be thankful for what we do have, to intentionally focus on what we can see and to keep on driving. And the good news is that the Lord our God promises that he will be with us.

I take great encouragement from the apostle Paul (a fairly impressive man of faith who contended with a barrel-load of suffering) and his words in Romans 5:2–5:

We boast in the hope of the glory of God. Not only so, but we also glory in our sufferings, because we know that suffering produces perseverance; perseverance, character; and character, hope. And hope does not put us to shame, because God's love has been poured out into our hearts through the Holy Spirit, who has been given to us.

It's important to note again that these incredible gems of perseverance, character and hope, these precious hallmarks of a resilient life, are produced by pressure, by stress and by suffering. But also, that this hope that we find is not dependent on or drawn from our own limited well of resources but is given to us as the endless love of God pours out and sustains us.

An Endurance Test

I think it would be fair to say that by the time we had met, Mark and I had both experienced a fair degree of stress. My parents had divorced rather acrimoniously during my teenage years. Mark's dad had died suddenly and because of this his family moved back to England from California. Having experienced these more weighty challenges individually, together we faced other trivial little hurdles like having absolutely no money, getting married quickly and moving across the country, with almost stoical acceptance.

But sometimes, even when you have built up fairly strong bounce-backable biceps, life throws you a heavy curveball that tests your endurance to the limits.

Digging for DIAMONDS

Mark had always found it difficult to see normally in low light, and when, after a year of marriage, we moved to London for Mark to take his degree in theology, he was referred to the local eye hospital (which happened to be one of the leading eye research centres in the country).

We were expecting a routine appointment, but after asking Mark about his sight and examining his eyes, the consultant asked us to wait in the consulting room while he popped out. When he returned, he was accompanied by a social worker with her guide dog, which we figured, being incredibly discerning, was not a good sign. Mark was gently told that his night-blindness was, in fact, the first symptom of a hereditary condition called Retinitis Pigmentosa, and that he would eventually lose his eyesight completely. A heavy diagnosis for a 25-year-old.

During that anything-but-routine appointment Mark was registered partially-sighted and was told he could no longer drive a car.

Another heavy weight.

A mere year afterwards, he was registered blind.

And another one.

Our resilience muscles ached, and our hopes and plans creaked under the stress. A significant bundle of questions would toss and turn in our minds, weighing us down and draining our emotional resources.

Perhaps you can relate in some way. Maybe you have had your own life-defining moment, which may have been totally out of your control but still changed the direction of your life.

Sometimes, for a variety of reasons, we find ourselves having to set up camp in a dark place for a while. It is not what we would have chosen. We didn't plan it, or seek it. But it is where we are. And without wishing to state the blatantly obvious, the darkness is not an easy place in which to live your life. No amount of reassuring words from others – promises that God wants to heal you/increase your faith/sort your problem out/teach you something (delete as appropriate) – or well-meant attempts to verbally fix your heartache, will ever make the darkness any less oppressive. In fact, on a bad day, some of those 'helpful' comments make you want to bless the contributors back with a holy punch in the face. In love, of course. We've heard it all over the years and I have often wondered whether people think that Jesus would add the kind of emotional guilt to the disabled, depressed or discouraged that we sometimes do.

The only theological certainty I know about suffering is this: God loves us and meets us in the midst of it. Again, God and life are not the same thing. We can't fully explain why everybody isn't healed or why some situations resolve and others don't. There isn't a scientific equation available and it isn't our responsibility to simplify it. But we do need a theological framework for suffering that recognises that God is with us in our darkest moments, and he knows what suffering feels like. It is of great significance and reassurance to me that it was a scarred Jesus who appeared to the disciples after the resurrection. It is a wounded saviour who breathes new life into us as we find our strength in him. God is our loving father who, rather than eliminating every obstacle and challenge from our lives, redeems our pain as we offer it to him. And we receive in return, through Christ, a resurrected hope.

Diamonds in the Darkness

Hope is the fuel that makes our journey possible. A few years after Mark's heavy diagnosis, I was away at a conference, and struggling (again) with letting go of so many hopes and dreams for our future. I also felt guilty for feeling such loss when Mark had so much more to cope with than me. But still, I longed for somebody to notice my new hairstyle or to be able to go to the cinema with me for a date. I missed sometimes being a passenger in the car and sharing a beautiful view with my husband. I wanted him, one day, to see his daughters in their wedding dresses. Is that so much to ask?

I thank God that the wonderful man speaking at the conference offered to pray with me and shared this verse from Isaiah which has given me hope and become a part of the fabric of my life:

> And I will give you treasures hidden in the darkness – secret riches. I will do this so you may know that I am the Lord, the God of Israel, the one who calls you by name.
>
> Isaiah 45:3, NLT

At that moment I saw with crystal clarity that treasures like diamonds are almost always found in the darkness. There are precious discoveries that will significantly enrich our lives which are normally hidden and can only be discovered as we plumb the depths. These treasures reveal to us more clearly than ever that God knows us and calls us

There are precious discoveries that will significantly enrich our lives which are normally hidden and can only be discovered as we plumb the depths.

and that his grace is sufficient for us – not just in theory or when things go well, but in our disappointment and our frustration too. I have yet to fully mine the riches of these verses, but you might be encouraged by the poem I wrote as I reflected upon them after that conference.

There are treasures in the darkness
Secrets to be shared
Truths to find, unexplored
Depths to plunge, unfathomed
Paths to follow, uncharted – until now
Will you travel close to me?

There are mysteries in misery
Riches past imitation
Without sight, there is vision
Without life, there is resurrection
Without words, liberation of spirit
Will your hand guide me?

There is providence in turbulence
Abandonment in the breeze

Digging for DIAMONDS

Where memory is precious
A touch cherished and savoured
A promise as real as a multi-faceted rainbow
Will your arms hold me steady there?

There is faith amidst confusion
A new sense unveiled
My tears held in your heavenly bottle
My future in your untainted focus
My worth more to you than shimmering jewels
Will you treat them tenderly?

There is trust wound around uncertainty
A hope that was hidden in fear
You who clustered constellations
Breathed blinding light into peace of night
Making belief profoundly simple
Will you show me the treasures of darkness?
Will you affirm my faltering discoveries?
Will you shine your glory through my story?
Will you love me even if I lose my way?
Will you?
Really?

I will step into your grace
I will find rest in your purposes
And I will take the time to treasure all I find.

It's still a frustrating journey, but I thank God that somehow Mark is still leading a church with his 4 per cent vision
and that we have, partly through a lack of any other option

but also through some deliberate choices, discovered the wonderful generosity of others, strength we didn't know we had and God's amazing grace.

Determination over Deviation

Part of developing our resilience is the determination not to deviate from the road and to keep driving. Somebody once said to me that if you can learn self-control you can learn anything, and there is some truth in that. If we give up giving up, it is amazing what we can achieve.

> If we give up giving up, it is amazing what we can achieve.

How many of us wish we hadn't quit piano lessons or regret that we didn't push through the pain barrier to do that charity race? We need a kind of holy stubbornness from time to time.

My daughter Naomi demonstrates this single-minded laser focus extremely well. In almost every pursuit, she doggedly perseveres until she achieves her goal. Mind you, it doesn't always work in her favour. A few years ago we stopped at a motorway service station and bought some chicken and chips. As she was pouring salt onto her already salty chips, I warned her that she probably had enough already. She looked at me and poured the entire contents out anyway. As I say, laser focus. She slowly and painfully ate her chips. Every mouthful looked like torture, and I watched smugly, as only a mother can. But it wasn't until much later that she confessed that she had mistakenly picked up packets of sugar instead of salt, and in so doing had created a sweet chip dish that was utterly revolting, but which she felt compelled to eat anyway. That determination will hopefully also mean that she is resilient when the going gets tough and she is tempted to give up on her studies, her relationships or her faith.

Not every challenge we face is out of our control. Sometimes we have a choice and a decision to make. There are occasions, both in the small and the large things where, as the saying goes, we will find an excuse or we will find a way. Some days procrastination wins over determination, I know, and it might not always be easy to keep going. But the risks of stalling or deviating from the road are just as challenging to face in the long term. So as Hebrews 12:1–2 reminds us, 'Let us run with perseverance the race marked out for us, fixing our eyes on Jesus, the pioneer and perfecter of faith.'

The Bible tells us that the power we need is from God, and not from ourselves, which is good news. I love how these verses remind us of the treasure of God that keeps us going when we want to get going. Paul tells us that our faith and our hope are like

Treasure from God, but we are like clay jars that hold the treasure. This shows that the great power is from God, not from us. We have troubles all around us, but we are not defeated. We do not know what to do, but we do not give up the hope of living. We are persecuted, but God does not leave us. We are hurt sometimes, but we

are not destroyed. We carry the death of Jesus in our
own bodies so that the life of Jesus can also be seen in
our bodies.

2 Corinthians 4:7–10, NCV

Our resilience and determination combined with our lack
of bitterness and cynicism are a wonderful witness to the
life of Jesus in us. Our vulnerability and honesty in the
midst of the dark places will give somebody else the confidence that there is hope. Our own struggles will equip
us as we comfort, support and pray for others. Just as
we are all challenged and inspired by people who have
endured far more in their lives than we could ever imagine, so our hurdles, no matter how big or small, can be
used by God as treasure to strengthen a fellow traveller.

Whatever your disability, challenges, grief or disappointment, God has not deserted you and will never
give up on you. In fact, it is as you hold on to him by
faith when everything else is falling away that you will
discover how deep his love really is. Mark's mum used
to have a poster in her kitchen of a kitten dangling in a
tree and holding on to the branch for its life. The words
above read, 'Faith isn't faith until it's all you're hanging
on to.' It is by faith that, as we endure despair, we will
find hope. By faith, we can move beyond failure to find
another chance to succeed. Beyond the bitter pain of
betrayal, with God, there can be a sweet story of forgiveness. Past the cross is a new and everlasting life. And we
need to hang on to it.

Digging for DIAMONDS

Even as you face the worst storms of this life, don't forget that God is still at work in you and is ultimately leading you towards a divine destination with a heavenly banquet in store.

So keep your eyes on him and keep driving.

DIGGING DEEPER

- Can you imagine, draw or write about the process by which diamonds are created under pressure? What impacts you in this creative meditation?

- When have you experienced 'good stress' that has been productive?

- When have you experienced the most challenging levels of stress, disappointment or fear?

- Is it possible that you ever confuse life with God? How do we focus upon the goodness of God in the storms of life?

- How honest and vulnerable are you to other people about your suffering? Is that a good thing?

- How much value do we as a church and individuals place on the 'resilience treasures' such as determination, perseverance, character and hope?

- What diamonds have you discovered in the darkness?

- How could God use your experiences to bring light to others?

King Jesus,

I thank you that you are the light of the world. Thank you that you stepped into the darkness, and that your perfect love casts out all fear. I trust that as I follow you, your word and your Spirit will illuminate my path, so that in good times and in bad I will learn to depend on you and know your presence. As I travel this road, use me to bless the lives of others along the journey, and to point to the hope that I have in you. Help me to keep on keeping on.

In your name and for your glory I pray,

Amen

CHARACTER

Chapter 7

HIDDEN

Set your minds on things above, not on earthly things. For you died, and your life is now hidden with Christ in God.

Colossians 3:2–3

There are, it seems to me, two types of people in the world: those who keep the contents of their drawers and cupboards tidy and those who don't. If you are one of the neat-aholics then, although we will never be friends, I am in awe of your skills. You believe inner peace is hung with your colour-coded clothes, folded with your ironed tea towels, stacked with your plastic containers and labelled with your electronic device chargers. Even your pets probably sit in size order. I'm pleased for you. If, however, you are a Chronic Clutter Collector, you might be able to pull off a semblance of order at Christmas, but woe betide anybody who dares to look behind any closed doors, because therein lies a mountain of stuff, precariously stacked and ready to avalanche at any moment.

I'm more on the CCC end of the spectrum myself. My children know if we are expecting guests because the vacuum cleaner gets dragged out from beneath the stairs. Most of the time we live in a messy muddle. But then every now and then something snaps in me and my psyche begins to scream, 'Enough already! I need to create order out of this chaos! I need a system and I need it NOW!' (Cue dramatic hand flourish.) Then I will take a trip to a Swedish furniture emporium, buy a trolley full of matchy matchy boxes and files, jars and shelves and create an oasis of inner calm expressed in outer Scandi-charm. Which lasts for, I don't know . . . about a week.

Once, while staying at the home of some friends in America, I saw a cross-stitch on the wall that read, 'If you want to see my house, make an appointment. If you want to see me, drop in any time.' That sums up my philosophy on household management pretty well. I'm not a total slob, but I do sometimes wonder whether my life would be a tiny bit more effective and a whole lot less stressed if what lurked beneath the surface was less jumble-sale-chic and more spick and span and ready for action.

Spiritually speaking, many of us also depend on a good spring clean from time to time. We cope with our dishevelled inner life for as long as possible and then make an annual pilgrimage to a festival or conference where we can focus, buy helpful resources and purposefully de-clutter and re-order our inner lives ready for the next season of chaos. Those experiences are always significant, and I attend some of those events every year, but sadly, they can fade all too quickly. Or perhaps we feel the benefit of the weekly spruce-up at church, where we can keep on top of the worst of our internal mess, despite the new bundle of challenges and opportunities that pile up every day. It's helpful and it's important, but it's still only going to get us so far.

In reality, our relationship with God and our character are formed, not only in those 'religious moments' where we expect God to be speaking, but in the equally holy moments of every day wherever we are. Just as it is a daily on-going ritual to keep a home tidy, so it is with our souls. It is not so much about occasionally trying hard, as training ourselves to practise regularly being in God's presence. He is always with us.

The geological-sounding truth is that everything that lies beneath the surface landscape of our lives shapes us, develops us and impacts the contours of the life that people can see. It is as we consciously connect with God more, and dig deeper into our thoughts and his presence, that we see more clearly what is visible and what is hidden, what we prioritise and what we neglect. What is hidden is always significant.

Underground Movement

Diamonds are hidden for almost all of their lives. They are formed deep in the earth's mantle, far from human eyes. Their value is forged in the depths of the planet, waiting patiently for millions of years before emerging through a volcanic eruption towards the surface. The hard work of crystallisation happens hidden from view, a long time before their beauty is ever revealed for the world to see.

Likewise, we only ever see a fraction of our oceans, icebergs or islands. We are only aware of a small percentage of all that is forming our visible world.

This process reminds me of the London Tube advertising campaign that said, 'All great movements begin underground.' It's true. Much of the activity we see around us was born in the recesses of the imagination of a passionate person, who then worked, believed and brought their vision to life. But although we see the end results, the most important part of that process is the invisible part. It shapes everything else to come.

Likewise, beneath the surface of our busy existence is the vital inner formation process that defines the contours of how we live. What is hidden is always deeply significant. Richard J. Foster, whose book *Celebration of Discipline* is regarded by many as a classic spiritual manual, says this: 'The desperate need today is not for a greater number of intelligent people, or gifted people, but for deep people.'[5]

> Beneath the surface of our busy existence is the vital inner formation process that defines the contours of how we live.

Ain't that the truth?

Do you ever feel like we are drowning in a shallow puddle? Our society sometimes feels like an orgy of superficiality. Everybody wants wisdom like diamonds, well-educated minds and finely honed skills, but most

[5]Richard J. Foster, *Celebration of Discipline: The Path to Spiritual Growth* (London: Hodder & Stoughton, 1980)

people don't really fancy doing the hard dirty work of digging to get there. They are busy people and there is another box set of an American series to watch, for goodness' sake. But who of us is immune? We admire the lives of successful business people or artists, but we would prefer not to make the sacrifices they have had to make to get where they are. Although we know that licking a talent into impressive shape is reputed to take 10,000 hours of practice and that a new habit apparently takes an average of 66 days to form, we hope that we will be the exception to the rule and we click to buy another book that promises us the easy steps to the success we crave.

But just as becoming a great public speaker, an accomplished pianist or an experienced engineer doesn't ever happen overnight, developing spiritual depth and maturity is also a long-term and largely hidden process. It might be that making a commitment to going deeper through spiritual self-discipline doesn't immediately sound like a whole load of fun to you. But when we keep our eyes on our goal, training is a purposeful and fulfilling activity, which although hard at times can also be exhilarating. Paul tells us in 1 Corinthians 9:25 that 'Everyone who competes in the games goes into strict training. They do it to get a crown that will not last, but we do it to get a crown that will last for ever.'

Although the extent of my daily exercise is walking down the stairs in the morning and back up them in the evening, I have many friends who are always training for one race or another, and pounding the streets whatever the weather. Their eyes are firmly on the prize. They know that the reward is worth having – they will be healthier and fitter and a charity will be richer if they just keep putting one foot in front of the other. And as inspiring as this is, Paul tells us that there also is a reward that lasts forever and it is our crown for keeping focused on Jesus and following him, come rain or shine.

It is right that others do not know everything about the extent of our training, which is hard in a world where we are addicted to sharing everything. It is for us to learn to wrestle in prayer and to study the Scriptures. We need to learn to fast, to spend time alone, to give secretly and to seek God in the mundane acts of service. These spiritual disciplines are largely hidden from the view of others but never hidden from God, and are a crucial part of becoming all we can be. If we want to be able to discern wisely, resolve conflict maturely and find peace in the midst of the chaos, then every sacrifice we make to grow in spiritual strength is worthwhile. And our prize is knowing the eternal presence of God, which will never disappoint us.

Deep Clean

The book of Hebrews also warns us that as we run the spiritual race, our own mistakes and sinful behaviour will inevitably tangle and trip us up (12:1). These hidden hurdles and secret obstacles, if left unchecked, get in the way of our relationship with God, and need to be brought into the open and dismantled in order for us to continue the race unhindered.

HIDDEN

Sometimes what is hidden needs exposing. About ten years ago, we had new windows and hardwood windowsills fitted into the bay windows of our Edwardian house. It was an expensive, messy and time-consuming process. So imagine my horror when one morning soon afterwards I came downstairs to find the word 'Daddy' engraved in biro onto one of those windowsills. As the family assembled, I looked my 5-year-old daughter intently in the eye.

'It wasn't me,' she said. 'It was my sister.' I looked over at her tiny 2-year-old sister who might have known how to chew a pen, but certainly didn't know how to write with it, and I looked back at the perpetrator. She knew that we knew. But it took a while for her to crack. Silly girl. Had she engraved the word 'Mummy' I might have been more lenient. Know which side your bread is buttered on, dear child. But as she looked down at the floor, apologised and admitted that her handwriting practice could probably be better expressed on paper, something happened: the atmosphere lifted, the truth was out in the open and our relationship of trust was restored.

Until she cut up her pyjamas a week later, anyway.

When we hide things we feel ashamed or guilty about, we own that shame. What you hide, you keep. It was Joseph Pulitzer, the newspaper publisher, congressman and namesake of the Pulitzer Prize who said, 'There is not a crime, there is not a dodge, there is not a trick,

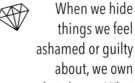

> When we hide things we feel ashamed or guilty about, we own that shame. What you hide, you keep.

there is not a swindle, there is not a vice which does not live by secrecy.'[6] Hidden secrets can be toxic. When we hide our struggles and misdemeanours beneath the surface, it slowly makes us sick, and the only remedy is to bring the truth out from the darkness and to disinfect and cleanse our hearts with the sunlight of God's grace.

The problem is that we all have a huge capacity for self-delusion. Let me demonstrate. My wardrobe has something in common with wardrobes up and down the land. Inside, it has a very small section of clothes that actually fit me, and an enormous rail of things that I believe I will wear again at some point in the future if, perhaps, I wire my jaws together. I am deluded. Fashion will have moved on by the time it ever happens, anyway. Here is the root of my madness: I know what I *say* I believe (that I will lose that stubborn weight), but it isn't what my actions would evidence that I *actually* believe (that I like doughnuts and sitting down).

What we do in reality reveals what we *really* believe, no matter what we say. I might tell you that I am on a diet or living on a budget, but if I find a way of telling myself the cake and the gadget is okay, then I am not really in control at all; I am on the fast lane to a guilt trip. I might say I care for the poor, but if I don't ever give or serve in a regular and sacrificial way, I probably just feel bad about knowing there are poor people. I might say I value a friendship, but if I don't spend any time building that relationship, then perhaps I don't really value it, after all. And I might declare

---

[6]Alleyne Ireland, *An Adventure with a Genius: Recollections of Joseph Pulitzer* (first ed. 1920)

that Jesus and his church are the hope of the world, but if I only rock up on a Sunday when the conditions are optimal, or speak dishonourably about it afterwards, then that declaration could legitimately be called into question. Do we say what we think we believe or do we dig deeper to discover what we really believe, and challenge ourselves to confess in order to bring things into the light and to grow?

There is a real need for clean hearts in this messy world – not messy hearts that we try to pass off to others (and ourselves) as clean enough. I might get away with trying to gently Febreze my soul, spraying my conscience with enough fragrance to give a good impression, but deep down, I need to be really clean. Jesus had a lot to say to the religious people in his generation who were able to sustain an exterior of scrupulous cleanliness while their inner attitudes and values were tainted. Although I don't aim to be pharisaic, I know that every day I do things to sabotage my clean slate. I make stupid choices that that stain my heart; I grasp at things that won't help me; I exaggerate and choose words that tear down instead of building up; I put myself before others and I put other things before God.

But believe me, brothers and sisters, I try not to let it show.

Which brings us to the privilege and the discipline of regular confession. We will never be perfect, and there is never any point pretending that we are. As we quieten our souls and listen to the Spirit, he will gently prompt us to confess our deepest fears and mistakes to God. He does this so that we can be released from our guilt as God removes the weight of our transgressions from us and banishes them as far as the east is from the west (Psalm 103:12).

As we confess and follow Jesus, he again offers us his living water that will realign our lives and cleanse us on the inside, because of his life, his death and his resurrection. It is pure, clean water that will purify us and hydrate our thirsty souls. Confession is not a discipline to be rushed or taken lightly, but with a humble and grateful heart, we need to daily drink and give thanks.

It is a deep clean.

Hidden in Christ

I remember once reading a kind of modern-day parable about a South African farmer who sold his farm to embark on a quest to search for diamonds. Unfortunately, although he travelled hundreds of miles, he never found the precious gems he was looking for. Very sadly, without a penny to his name, he finally jumped into a river and drowned. His dream had ended in despair. A few years later, however, the man who had bought the farmer's land found an unusual-looking rock. Upon examination by a friend it was discovered that the rock was, in fact, the biggest diamond that had ever been found. That farm was transformed into the Kimberley Diamond Mine – the richest and probably the best known mine in the world. [7]

Here was a man who was prepared to give his life for something that he did not know he already had. He had

[7]Told by Dr Keith Warrington in *Hope Distance Learning Course* by Regents Theological College

no idea of the value of what was already hidden under his feet and therefore he didn't spend any time looking for it. It's a tragedy to think that what was beneath the surface of his own land could have changed his life, if only he had truly owned what was already below him.

This contrasts with another parable about hidden treasure (Matt. 13:44), where Jesus tells us, 'The kingdom of heaven is like treasure hidden in a field. When a man found it, he hid it again, and then in his joy went and sold all he had and bought that field.'

This man, unlike the first, does find treasure in a field and, being pretty sure that it will change his life forever, endeavours to do whatever is necessary to bring the bling back. Isn't it interesting how

> If we find something of worth that we perceive will change our lives, then we will invest in it and cherish it.

the behaviour of these two men is completely driven by their perception of the value of their field? If we find something of worth that we perceive will change our lives, then we will invest in it and cherish it. If it's a new phone, we will invest in it. If it's a house, we will invest in it – especially if it has a field. But the treasure Jesus is referring to is the kingdom of God. You can't buy it and you are not likely to stumble upon it, but when you find it, it is worth everything.

Isn't it extraordinary to think that while we could be searching the world for contentment, what we really want is simply hidden in our own back yard waiting to be found? Freedom. Forgiveness. Justice. Hope. Purpose. Priceless treasures, hidden in the overgrowth of our often uncultivated culture, waiting to be discovered and cherished.

As followers of Jesus, these treasures are already ours. The riches of the kingdom of God are there for us to steward and to share – which is pretty incredible if you stop to think about it. Jesus has set up residence in the field of our heart and Paul tells the Colossians (3:3) that we are 'hidden with Christ'. Everything good is wrapped up in him and in him we find all we need.

> My goal is that they may be encouraged in heart and united in love, so that they may have the full riches of complete understanding, in order that they may know the mystery of God, namely, Christ, in whom are hidden all the treasures of wisdom and knowledge.
>
> Colossians 2:2–3

As we deliberately encourage each other to delve beneath the surface and unearth these diamonds, we will discover more of God's plans for our lives. As we explore the word of God, we will grow in wisdom. As we worship and pray persistently, learning to enjoy his presence, we will glimpse his glory. As we consistently love, give and serve, we will discover how to depend upon his power. As each of us embrace our place of solitude, we will discover through prayer, reading, meditation or journaling, the wonders of the deep. I don't know about you, but I want to discover those treasures and I also want to spend time with people who have been digging deeper for longer and who have discovered the treasures in their own back yard.

Deeper and Further

Looking beyond the surface extends beyond our own introspection. As we begin to think deeper, we realise that whatever people present us with, something else is always going on beneath the surface. Usually, the stronger the reaction we get from people, the more questions we need to ask. In our church we often talk about the OFM (One Fact More) principle. It transforms situations. One more piece of information can reframe what we initially see completely. When we interact with people, watch the news or learn about decisions that have been made, there are always things that we just don't know. Instead of judging superficially, it pays to ask for One Fact More. Depth of understanding always makes a difference. Was that person being grumpy or had they actually just suffered a huge personal grief you know nothing about? One Fact More. Did your new colleague just totally ignore you or does he have a hearing problem and depend on lip reading? One Fact More.

Similarly, as we work, live and shop as disciples of Jesus, we begin to ask deeper questions about issues such as the ethics of the supply chain we support or the effects of our actions on other people and the environment. We realise that what is hidden matters. What lies beneath the surface shapes what is visible. We can only make a difference to individual lives and to the larger issues of justice or oppression when we begin to explore what we don't immediately see. It takes some effort, but it's an incredibly rewarding thing to be a part of reshaping the landscape around us.

> Prioritising depth over breadth is never a waste of time.

Digging for DIAMONDS

Excavation is always worthwhile. Prioritising depth over breadth is never a waste of time. The truth is, the more we live on the surface, the more we lose touch with what is going on deep inside us and others. The adventure of faith is found as we break ground and discover the diamonds that God has given us, and allow them to shape the landscape of our life.

The treasure is already ours, but there's always more to discover.

DIGGING DEEPER

- Have you ever seen a volcano or thought about how deep our planet is as we live on its surface? Do a quick Internet search to discover more about where diamonds are formed.

- Are you a neat freak or a clutter collector? To what extent does the appearance of your house reflect what is hidden behind the scenes?

- What are your spiritual habits? Do you occasionally spring clean, regularly clear the decks or systematically keep your heart in order?

- What aspects of our shallow culture do you find most distracting? Do you ever delude yourself about that or justify your actions?

- Are you more prone to trying harder or training smarter? How could your spiritual training be improved?

- Is confession something you feel at home with? How best could you ensure you are regularly deep cleaned before God?

- How can you increasingly treasure the riches that are hidden in Christ?

- This week, where could you look deeper beneath the surface? In the lives of others? In the bigger issues? Try the OFM principle.

Heavenly Father,

I thank you for the words of Psalm 42 that say that 'deep calls to deep'. This is the cry of my heart today, Lord, to go past the shallows into the deep waters of knowing you. I thank you that you see everything that is hidden in me, good and bad, and you love me completely. I confess again the things I have done that I should have walked away from, and the things I should have done but didn't. Cleanse me, Lord. Create in me a new heart. Meet me as I practise being in your presence and explore the riches found hidden in you. Save me from the shallows, and help me to create a landscape that reveals the kingdom of God.

In your precious name I pray,

Amen

Chapter 8

AUTHENTIC

Whoever walks in integrity walks securely, but whoever takes crooked paths will be found out.

Proverbs 10:9

I recently experienced what you might call 'a slight mishap'.

I was eagerly munching through a pile of fancy pastries in a hotel in Chester, where a colleague and I were having breakfast with a wonderful local businessman. It was all very civilised. Our new friend announced that he had a treat in store for us – or rather a treat in a store, which was next door and owned by a friend of his.

'Nice,' I thought. 'Shopping is good.'

The establishment in question, however, turned out to be none other than Boodles, one of the most exclusive jewellers in the land, and we were going to get to meet the team and hold some of their collection of diamonds and precious stones which have been personally sourced and set into uniquely designed jewellery for discerning customers who have the kind of money that can buy you Hampshire.

Digging for DIAMONDS

I should have made a run for it there and then.

I was still vigorously dusting croissant crumbs from my jeans as I walked past the security guards into one of the most beautiful shops I have ever seen. I successfully fought back the temptation to squeal and clap my hands with glee as I took in the gleaming glass cabinets filled with stunning sparkling jewels.

After I had spent a few minutes drooling and then rocking subtly back and forth on their very cool reclining chairs, one of the staff passed me a particularly beautiful necklace to admire. At its heart was a ruby with a colour so bright that it seemed to dance. Around this ruby looped sinuous swirls of diamonds, intricately set, with a large shimmering diamond droplet resting beneath the whole design. I held it in my hands, in no small amount of awe and admiration. I rested it delicately upon my knee as I examined its craftsmanship. I marvelled at its beauty and considered how incredible it was that this piece of jewellery cost more than my house. And then it happened. In one slow-motion moment of mortification, I watched that masterpiece slide unceremoniously from my knee and crumple onto the floor.

Awkward. I mean, really, very awkward. Awkwardus Maximus.

Fortunately, the polite and lovely staff, clearly trained for any clumsy eventuality, responded with utter charm, and as I left, lobbing a Boodles brochure into my bag (just in case, one never knows), I reflected again upon just how incredibly beautiful and valuable these precious stones are, and what a privilege it would be to own any of them.

The Genuine Article

When you are fortunate enough to own or even to try on a piece of genuine jewellery with diamonds that have been painstakingly mined, cut, polished and designed, you know that you are wearing something exceptional. None of this cubic zirconia business. Although across a dimly lit room your mass-produced fake might sparkle in a similar way to your one-off gem, you would, I hope, treat it in a completely different way. For instance, you probably wouldn't install a safe in your house for a cheap reproduction ring. You wouldn't bother to get it insured or reserve wearing it for a really special occasion. No, we value the genuine article in a totally different way to an imitation.

It's no surprise, then, that we appreciate people who are the real deal as well. We admire those who live out their beliefs with integrity, and we are inspired by the Mother Teresas and Nelson Mandelas of this world. When we spend time with a person who is authentic and genuine, we feel we are in the presence of somebody who is the same through and through, like you'd find if you broke a seaside stick of rock in half. We value the qualities of those who are true to themselves, wherever they are.

I can't help but love the upfront honesty of Dolly Parton, who, with her usual wit, said, 'It's hard to be a diamond in a rhinestone world.' While I am told that apparently not everything about

> We value the qualities of those who are true to themselves, wherever they are.

her physique is absolutely natural, she is undoubtedly

a woman who has with honesty, humour and talent created her own path from the humble two-bedroom cabin in the Smoky Mountains of her childhood. She is entirely comfortable with being herself, in her own way, despite what others may say about her. She's even real about what isn't completely real about her, which I find refreshing in a quirky kind of way.

The truth is, even when you are an original in a rhinestone world, some people will accuse you of being a fake. In fact, people are more likely to notice you when you step out of the crowd and have the confidence to do things your own way, dress in your own style, take a career that nobody expected, make radical decisions or serve where others fear to tread. Less pioneering people may well be suspicious about your motives or even cause others to doubt your credentials.

But why not do a Dolly and decide to rock your own style anyway? The world will always have a surplus of imitators and commentators, ready to copy and critique, but those whom we value the most are the ones who find the freedom to be themselves.

Reality Check

Of course, it's not always easy to spot an original. Experts spend years examining paintings in order to discover the true hand of the artist, or they meticulously check antique furniture and jewellery for signs of wear and tear. But it seems that people are a bit trickier. In our celebrity-obsessed, success-driven, instant culture, where image becomes reality and you fake it till you make it, how do we even know if people are being true to themselves? Are there telltale signs that somebody is, you know, a bit stingy in the honesty department?

A couple of years ago, while the council was replacing the tarmac on the road outside our house, a man with a high-vis jacket and an official-looking, photo-laden council lanyard knocked on our door and asked us if we wanted to employ the lads to use some of the leftover materials to repair our tired driveway. Apparently, he said, a few of the neighbours had already agreed and it was all quite normal. Even as I write, I can see now how ridiculous this was. He sounded, you must understand, so nice, so incredibly trustworthy.

The next day, he and his team turned up to our house with a battered truck, a few brooms and a vat of mucky dark stuff (not a council-level piece of equipment in sight). I knew I had been royally duped, so I set about transforming myself into Miss Marple. I surreptitiously took photographs from the windows, asked specific and leading questions and jotted down number plates. From behind my twitching curtain I called the Trading Standards Institute and could practically hear them wringing their hands with joy as I provided them with evidence against a bunch of crooks they had been trying to take to court for years.

They wasted no time in acting. Those boys were arrested and prosecuted, fake council badges and all. I'm just grateful that I wasn't also arrested – for illegal levels of gullibility. Perhaps I should have remembered the old adage, 'If it looks too good to be true, then it probably is.'

Digging for DIAMONDS

But sometimes a fake can actually be quite impressive. For example, experts tell us that fine paste (imitation) emeralds can actually appear better than inferior genuine emeralds. In fact, paste jewellery, far from being derided, was regarded as an art form, hugely popular with the royalty and aristocracy of the Georgian and Victorian times. The jewellers of the day, who traded in these completely artificial gems, which were literally too good to be true, became extraordinarily wealthy men.

It is possible for us not only to be impressed or dazzled by what is not entirely genuine, but to create an entire industry out of it. In an odd inversion of reality, our society often constructs a new kind of authentic or acceptable out of what was previously obscure or implausible. For instance, our screens are awash with blogs, videos and episodes of the many TV 'reality' shows that are often evidence enough that it is possible to fabricate a career, a personality or an image out of the most abstract raw materials.

> It is possible for us not only to be impressed or dazzled by what is not entirely genuine, but to create an entire industry out of it.

But no matter how good or compelling an imitation is, everybody, deep down, wants the real deal. Do you remember the 1969 advert telling us that Coca-Cola is the real thing? I'm obviously far too young to have been there at the time (okay, it's close) but I still recognise it and for years thought this was purely a great example of marketers' blurb. And then I met my husband. Yes, Mark can identify the taste of fake Coke in a nanosecond (I know, I've tried just for fun).

He would rather drink mouthwash than consume a diet version or replacement brand of the cola-nectar. Some people get sniffy over the provenance of their wine; others turn their noses up at instant coffee. But for Mark, it really is all about that sickly sweet brown stuff, and he only wants the so-called 'real thing'.

In a similar way, we experience an unpleasant taste when people are less than genuine with us. We hurt when a friend doesn't tell us the truth or a spouse lets us down. We're disappointed when we discover that a pop star can't really sing or a journalist has twisted the truth. We're devastated to learn that a politician has lived a double life or a police officer has expressed racist views. No matter how impressive or persuasive people appear to be, we all yearn for relationships and role models that are the real thing. We long

> We long for those who are strong enough to be vulnerable about who they really are.

for those who are strong enough to be vulnerable about who they really are and not simply who they would like us to believe they are. I think the wisdom of Proverbs 10:9 sums it up nicely: 'Whoever walks in integrity walks securely, but whoever takes crooked paths will be found out.'

A lack of authenticity will be discovered, sooner or later, and it never tastes good.

A Holiness Highway

It takes guts to be authentic. Our desire to be our genuine self must outweigh our fear of not being liked or being different. It's not always easy sticking to what we know is right or what we know God has asked of us, especially when the crowd surges in a different direction. But Jesus tells us we have a choice to make: 'Enter through the narrow gate. For wide is the gate and broad is the road that leads to destruction, and many enter through it. But small is the gate and narrow the road that leads to life, and only a few find it' (Matt. 7:13–14).

Every time I read this passage, I am reminded of a particular morning when I dropped my two teenage daughters off at a gate at the front of the school.

'Oh great,' one of them said. 'Now we are going to have to walk.'

'No,' I replied, 'I think you will find I have dropped you off right next to the school gate.'

'Oh Mum,' she said with a disparaging glare from behind her school bag. 'Nobody cool would ever use this gate.'

I looked over at my other daughter for support, but she just nodded sagely as my mouth gaped open. Could they even be serious? How were these talented, determined, creative young women ever going to find the strength to define their own groove in the world if they couldn't even walk through a supposedly uncool gate?

The truth is, we all want to walk through the cool gate. None of us want to be the person wandering around on their own, wishing somebody would invite us to their party. And the emotional magnet that tugged our adolescent selves so hard it could have given gravity a run for its money still gives us the odd yank as adults. But the cool gate isn't always everything it's cracked up to be. It might seem splendid initially to walk a well-trodden path, where everybody apparently moves in the same direction, but choosing the adventure of faith is far more exciting.

With the Holy Spirit as our guide, and the word of God as a lamp to our feet, we walk in the Way. As Isaiah 35:8 tells us, 'A highway will be there; it will be called the Way of Holiness; it will be for those who walk on that Way.' Others might think we are a little bit barmy to go through the narrow gates of loving when it's hard – giving sacrificially or stepping out in faith when we are unsure of the outcome – but we're walking through the gates that lead to a highway of holy living, where we can discover precious truths about God while exploring places we would never have thought possible with people who have chosen to go off the beaten track together.

Imagine, if you will, that you're walking through a forest on a beautiful sunny day. The trees wave in the breeze and your feet crunch along the wide gravel path beneath your shoes. But then, to the side of the path, you see a small trail leading off into the woods, not formally laid out or marked, but winding casually into the distance. Are you as intrigued by this new path as I would be?

I found out about these small winding paths through my husband Mark who, when researching for a sermon, discovered that these unmarked trails that go off the beaten track are called 'desire paths'. They are called this because when you see them, you experience a desire to explore, a yearning to go down them, a curiosity to know more. I love finding these paths, and even if I get a little lost as I meander along them, it is an exquisite pleasure to find unexpected clearings carpeted with bluebells or old empty trees that children can clamber onto.

It might take a bit of courage to do our own thing and walk through the potentially uncool gate or down the uncharted narrow path to follow our desires, our dreams and our conscience. But as we step out in faith, so we become more aware of the truth of God and the promptings of the Holy Spirit, and we are drawn deeper, away from the ruts of making the right impression or doing what others do, onto a path where we discover the delights of truly authentic living.

Authentic Originals

The dictionary tells us that if something is authentic it is of undisputed origin. As we strip back the layers of status, ego or busyness, we begin to discover again that, at our core, we have originated from God. Nothing could be more impressive or important than knowing that the Creator of the Universe knows us and loves us as authentic originals. Yet sometimes we behave as if this is not status enough.

Most of us would not deliberately set about being fake or artificial, but many of us would prefer other people to see an ever-so-slightly better version of ourselves than we know is the truth. We so want people to know and love the real and genuine us but we feel a little vulnerable about the warts-and-all version, so we rub on a little polish in the hope that we might be a little more likeable. Whether

We so want people to know and love the real and genuine us but we feel a little vulnerable about the warts-and-all version.

it is through social media or face to face, we can so easily give the impression that we are a little more spiritual than we are, a bit more in control of our finances than we are, slightly fitter than we are, and oh the list goes on . . .

Rub, rub, rub. Polish, polish, polish . . .

In church, the one place where in theory we should be more real than anywhere else, week by week people pretend they are just fine, instead of being vulnerable and showing their true selves. Perhaps we think that unless we have it all together, we somehow aren't living a victorious Christian life. If so, it might help to go back to the Bible and read about those who have gone before us. For instance, Paul did not live a charmed life. When he talked about having to learn to be content in all situations, he was not writing from Hawaii sipping a Pina Colada, he was in prison. Even Jesus, the ultimate in authenticity, cried and felt hurt and disappointed amidst the friendships and the miraculous. So why would we pretend to each other that life is better than it is or grumble that it is worse than it is? (It seems we usually fall more easily into one of those camps.)

Our purpose, being together as disciples, is to focus again on God, the originator of our faith, and his word, and then to work out authentically the reality of our life together so that we might be equipped for service and be strengthened through every circumstance together. It will require a definite commitment to honesty, vulnerability and patience, alongside an extremely well-developed sense of humour.

But you know, it is a particular tragedy when those in leadership in the church (or any context), through pressure or frailty, end up living a life of inauthenticity. When we see apparently strong marriages end in tatters or when addiction or corruption take root in the life of a significant leader, the results are always devastating. Perhaps most upsetting of all, our children look around and wonder who is really telling the truth around here. And so, in our hearts, do we.

I'll be honest – it isn't always a picnic living in the goldfish bowl of ministry, with eyes watching you all the time and commenting on your swimming style. I'm not going to deny that at times our public family face hasn't exactly matched the reality of our experience.

There have been weeks when there has been tension before we have got into the car to drive to church, along the journey to church and as we have screeched into the church car park. My children have sometimes observed a transformation so miraculous as I exit the car and walk into the church building that they stand still in awe, watching as my tense frown melts into a smile and I ask everybody about how their week has been. Fortunately, our family likes to laugh about this rapid metamorphosis quite a lot (that is, they laugh at me mainly), and Mark and I have made the strategic and life-enhancing decision not to speak to each other on a Sunday morning. It works for us.

But that's not just true for ministry families, right?

Living in Line

In a hundred little choices that you and I will make today, we have the opportunity to show the kind of integrity and authenticity that declares that we want our life to line up with what we believe and who we are, wherever we are.

So, do we say 'fine' when we are asked how we are or do we share appropriately the challenges we face or the moments that have made us sing with joy? Do we get impatient with every person who dares to share the road with us on the way to work or do we extend the kind of grace we would like to receive in return? Do we say yes to every request we receive in life or do we listen to ourselves and to God and follow the path we know is right for us?

When we know that we are good enough in God's eyes to be our original selves, and that he is with us, then we will live in the freedom this brings. We can paint our lounge orange if we want to or listen to madrigals all day if that is our thing. We can build a career or live by faith, as we feel it is right to do. Just as we admire and respect that confidence in others, so others will respond to us accordingly. In fact, a good friend once told me that we train others in the way we want them to treat us, and she is right about that. When we are comfortable with being ourselves and confident about the path we have chosen, the people around us will trust us and know that we are true to our word.

Living in line with who we really are is a beautiful and a valuable asset. We put a high price on something that we know to be genuine. We need to keep on keeping it real.

Because authenticity matters.

DIGGING DEEPER

- Can you tell the difference between a real diamond and a cubic zirconia? If you have one of each, how do you treat them differently?

- Which people come to your mind when you think of being the real deal (public role models as well as people you know)? Why did you think of them?

- How do you know whether people are people of integrity? Have you ever been misled?

- How confident are you about choosing the narrow gate or desire paths? Do you find it easy to be different or do you tend to follow the crowd?

- How consistently do you give an accurate impression to other people about yourself? Why?

- How do you balance the need to be appropriate about what you share with whom, with being real wherever you are?

- What would living authentically look like for you in the week ahead?

Lord God, originator of everything good,

I thank you that you are always constant and faithful. I thank you that in a world where not everything or everybody is always reliable, you are my rock and my fortress. I pray that I would have the courage to be authentically all you have made me to be and that I would grow in the love of Christ. Help me to walk in the freedom of knowing that I am yours and have been made to reflect your glory in my own authentic way.

In the name of Jesus,

Amen

Chapter 9

LAVISH

And my God will meet all your needs according to the riches of his glory in Christ Jesus.

Philippians 4:19

It has been a very exciting year for our community. Oh yes, indeed. Our local middle-of-the-road supermarket ceased being a middle-of-the-road supermarket and had a fabulous facelift. I know. After months of anticipation, there it proudly stood. Gone was the old scruffy brand and here was the shiny new reincarnated Waitrose. Bye bye old shoddy doors; hello fabulous entrances. Good riddance naff stuff; welcome shabby-chic garden accessories. The social-media activity in the area was nothing short of frenetic. Even the conversations after church were enthusiastic expressions of awe and admiration at the delights of free coffee and the divine deli bar. Naturally, I was curious to visit and experience this heavenly place in our midst, and when I did, I could only watch in wonder as previously rather average shoppers were now to be found flouncing down the aisles, latte in hand, considering the benefits of organic pasta. What a transformation!

As I grabbed my complimentary coffee and newspaper (who am I to argue?) and backed out of the door, I realised that my problem is that I am at heart a child of the seventies. When you were brought up on a diet of Brain's Faggots, Findus Crispy Pancakes and Angel Delight, there's no hope of feeling genuinely posh. What was going on in the seventies anyway? What were the makers of Smash (gag), sweet tinned carrots and fruit cocktail even thinking? Perhaps it was a reaction to the migraine-inducing colour-crazed fashion and interiors of the decade, but our food was beige, bland and bad, with a good dollop of tomato ketchup or its exotic summer sister, salad cream, on the side. In our home, we bought 'posh' food once a year – at Christmas, when glamorous arrivals like satsumas and dates (that nobody dared to eat) appeared on the coffee table. And as for eating out – well that really was a rare treat. Partly, I am guessing, because there was nowhere much to go apart from getting a bag of fish and chips in proper newspaper or (brace yourself) visiting the smelly smoky local pub where we children would be cast into a dingy kids' room out the back with a packet of cheese and onion crisps while the adults had what I can only assume was a rip-roaring time in the bar.

How times have changed. Contrast those depressed years to our shiny and fabulous high streets now, with a coffee shop or a family-friendly restaurant every ten paces. Observe the children munching on their chorizo flatbreads and sipping on their babycinos. We are a big self-indulgent leap away from forty years ago.

And, it's worth bearing in mind, a world away from most of the world today.

A few years ago Mark and I visited Africa with our two girls. I had been hesitating about taking them. It's quite a thing to allow your children to face the startling poverty that we would encounter as we visited the charity we had worked with as a church for a few years. As we considered the trip I asked the head of the charity, at what age did he think it was appropriate to take children to see the reality of life for so many people in Africa? He looked me straight in the eye and said, 'About the same age that you start taking them to shopping malls.' Okay then.

We booked the tickets.

On that trip we met people, as poor as you could realistically be, who welcomed us, sat on their floor with us and shared songs of thanksgiving and praise with us. They were by no means rich economically speaking, but they had a deep conviction that their worth was rooted in being loved and loving others. I will never forget one lady, ill and frail as she was, getting up and going outside to pick one of the mangos from her almost bare garden to give to me. I felt utterly undeserving and deeply concerned that she was giving something so precious away. But our friend who works with the charity held it out to me and reminded me that although this lady had spent months watching this mango grow, it was her pleasure to be able to share it with me. I can still close my eyes and recall those smiling faces, the impact of that simple act of outrageous generosity and the taste of the sweetest mango in the entire world.

A Culture of 'More'

We can't (and wouldn't want to) de-clutter everything from our lives to live in poverty, but somehow we must liberate ourselves from the addiction to 'more' and learn what it means to be lavish towards others with what God has already extravagantly given us.

While our society elevates self-gratification to a national pastime, we are called to think differently. Our time and our resources are given to us for us to steward wisely and to bless others with, as well as to enjoy ourselves. This is not just a good thing to do, or a top tip for being a nice person; Jesus spoke a lot about what we value and how we manage our possessions and money. A surprising amount, actually. There was more commentary from the Son of God about our attitude to stuff than about prayer and the kingdom of God put together. Jesus knew how our lust for affluence can be a real barrier to our spiritual growth and reminded us that we cannot serve the two masters of God and money at the same time (Matt. 6:24).

> Understanding how we live in the context of our belongings is important spiritual business.

For us all, understanding how we live in the context of our belongings is important spiritual business. Much of the character and the spiritual depth we admire in others is mirrored by their attitude and focus towards what they own and who benefits from what God has given them.

But it's not easy is it? The constant pressure to maintain our lives and our credit card bills has never been greater. According to the Centre for Social Justice, household debt in the UK has doubled in the last decade. While for many people simply paying the bills can be a struggle, it is also true that the treadmill of acquiring more and then counting the cost can anaesthetise us from connecting with what our real needs are. I once saw a young man being interviewed, who described us as living 'in the amniotic fluid of consumerism'. It is almost like the air we breathe. Our value has become so closely linked to our lifestyle that we are forever 'needing' something more. I shop, therefore I am. I take selfies in front of beautiful views, therefore I am. I eat fabulous meals, therefore I am.

Richard Foster reminds us how crazy this can make us:

> 'We really must understand that the lust for affluence in contemporary society is psychotic. It is psychotic because it has completely lost touch with reality. We crave things we neither need nor enjoy. We buy things we do not want to impress people we do not like . . . It is time to awaken to the fact that conformity to a sick society is to be sick.'[8]

Some of us are more badly afflicted by this issue than others. The chances are you are naturally either a saver or a spender. And if you are married to or friends with the opposite of the species, the differences between you could quite possibly cause some tension. My husband Mark is a saver. Every year, he embarks upon an Olympian

[8]Richard J. Foster, *Celebration of Discipline*

quest to save money on our various insurances and every year he goes on a short shopping expedition to buy an identical replacement pair of jeans that he will wear out over the following twelve months. He knows how much we spend on absolutely everything and, thanks to his financial savvy, we have been able to accomplish amazing things on a limited income.

It probably won't surprise you to know that he really doesn't understand why I buy stuff. I come home with another cushion or (ouch) another pair of shoes and he looks at me as if I am one of the greatest mysteries of the universe. He saves his birthday money for years until he can afford a gadget he really wants and can't quite figure out how I have always spent my birthday money months before my actual birthday because I have found something on special offer. I am (she remarks defensively), actually quite careful with money and am never reckless, but nevertheless I know that I get the same pleasure from coming home with a new book as he does from balancing the books. We are just wired completely differently.

So, is one of us right and one of us wrong? Not so much. We each have things to learn from each other, but we also face different temptations. I could, if I let myself go, spend far more than we have on things we don't need or even carelessly give away more than we could afford. Mark, in contrast, could, if left unchecked, become a walking budgetary discipline department who might never spend money on anything superfluous or resent the cost of a restaurant meal even when he is eating it.

The key thing is this: whether we are talking about our money, our time, our creativity, our smile, our words or our home – everything we have comes from God. Everything. And so, everything we have has the potential to glorify God and to reflect the extravagant love he has shown us. When we are able to both look after what we have been given carefully *and* share it generously, it gives God as much pleasure as it gives us. If you are a parent, you know that when your kids look after their possessions and when they share or are kind, your heart just swells. God loves it when we both discipline ourselves and walk in the freedom of generous living that is made possible by that self-discipline. We need to make good choices so that we are free to make other good and exciting choices.

Simple Generosity

Most of us would agree that we have more than we need. The antidote to the relentless pursuit of more is for us to deliberately choose less. Simplicity is the only way to counteract excess. So, recently I set myself a challenge: can I pay equal or even more attention to what I already have than to what I do *not* have, so that I begin to see the worth in what is already around me? Could I rediscover and enjoy what is already mine? Could I resist looking at what more I could want for a while? It is perfectly possible for us to inadvertently skim over the value of the relationships, the gadgets or the belongings that we already have, instead

> The antidote to the relentless pursuit of more is for us to deliberately choose less.

of stopping to notice and appreciate them with fresh gratitude. But God is not the one cracking the whip and asking us to always work harder, accumulate more or keep up with the wealthiest and trendiest of our friends. Throughout the Bible, the general principles we learn are to earn ethically, to spend wisely, to save carefully and to give regularly and sacrificially. These principles are not a straitjacket, sucking the spontaneity out of life; they are, in fact, real keys to freedom and a generous and satisfying life.

The root of our motivation is a fresh realisation that our entire life is an act of worship to God. We are called to respond to him without holding back, which is easier to sing on a Sunday than it is to do. But even on a Sunday, it is often a decision to give God the lavish worship he deserves. I remember a particular time when I was struggling to mentally connect or express any emotion during the musical worship at church. I just wasn't feeling it. And while it is normal for our experience of worship to ebb and flow, a good friend who leads a wonderful church asked me an insightful question: he asked me how long it would take for me to say 'I love you' to Mark if I always waited for my feelings to prompt me. (He somehow guessed that we don't always exist in a warm cocoon of romantic fuzziness.) Then he told me that it is often as we deliberately choose to say the words that the feelings and thoughts follow, rather than the other way round. He is so right. Both in our relationship with others and with God, it is often as we choose to reach out, to physically and verbally act and express ourselves, that the emotional and intellectual connection happens. Is God worth reaching out to? Is he worthy of our focused and extravagant worship, despite our feelings? He is. Just as Mary poured out a year's worth of wages in a bottle of perfume over Jesus as a lavish act of adoration, so we must find our own way of pouring out an offering of worship to a God who has given so extravagantly to us.

We can never outgive God. Turning our attention to him is a sure-fire way of breaking our dependency on self-centredness. And as we fix our eyes on him and his word, we will instinctively begin to look around and see other people and the world through his eyes. The most important commandment, Jesus tells us in Mark 12:30–31, is to 'Love the Lord your God with all your heart and with all your soul and with all your mind and with all your strength,' and the second is to 'Love your neighbour as yourself.'

All of your heart. All of your soul. All of your mind. All of your strength. This is the kind of wholehearted and lavish love that immediately ripples out and expresses itself in caring for other people just as much as we care for ourselves. Our worship should always lead us to adjust our focus onto the world. And then, as we love and serve others, that is also a part of our devotion to God. It's a kind of virtuous circle. Jesus said that when we feed the hungry or look after the sick or welcome the stranger it is as if we are doing it to him. When you bake that cake or smile at that shop assistant or listen to a struggling friend, you are touching the heart of Jesus. Your worship leads you to love others, which is also worship.

Extravagant Love

And what happens when we are on the receiving end of unexpected and unrestrained love from others? We almost always feel so blessed that we want to make somebody else feel as deeply touched as we do.

Earlier this year my eldest daughter and I went away for a weekend as a reward for all of her pre-exam hard work. We stayed with some friends who lived close to the area we wanted to visit. There is no doubt that God has blessed this couple as they have worked hard. Their business has grown and their house is a stunning place to call home. But, as a person once said to me, it is not how many rooms you have, but what you do with them that matters. This house was humming with the sound of teenagers visiting for a BBQ, a church girls' group playing in the garden and work colleagues staying overnight. The amount of people being welcomed and the mountain of food that was being prepared would have been more than enough to give me a nervous breakdown had it been my house. But no. We were treated like visiting royalty. We had a fabulous Chinese meal by candlelight, an afternoon tea in a hotel and were even lent a little soft-top sports car to drive around the countryside. These wonderful people had the creativity and the resources to make our weekend more special than we ever could have imagined. We were expecting a bed and a box of cornflakes. We were abundantly blessed.

So what did Naomi and I talk about as we drove home, apart from the delights of the weekend? We discussed how we could use more of what we have to make people feel that special. While we don't have the space and money that our friends have, we do have a lovely house, a great garden and more food than we need. This makes us incredibly fortunate. So, instead of our home simply being a sanctuary or a retreat for us, we discussed how it could increasingly be a place of welcome where we can creatively and generously bless others, showing them how valuable they are.

For years I had a mental block about hospitality. I would worry endlessly about the dust and dirty dishes and I would stress myself silly about what to cook, as if it was about impressing people. But we don't need our house to be like an interior from a magazine, and it's not about the food either. Until recently, we have had a friend over most Thursday nights as a part of our family meal. It started during a painful time of separation and divorce for her but the tradition lasted for years. We loved seeing her and she happily tucked into the sausages and mash or spaghetti bolognese that got served up after we had rushed in from school rehearsals. None of us were awarded Michelin stars, and some weeks she strolled into chaos, but we shared some profound moments of joy and some days of deep despair as we sat around our dining table together.

> Being lavish and generous and others-focused is not about how much we have to give, so much as giving what we have.

Being lavish and generous and others-focused is not about how much we have to give, so much as giving what we have. It is interesting to note that there is no relationship between the size of a diamond and the pleasure it gives to the person receiving it. Diamonds have been an extravagant expression of love and commitment since roughly the end of the fifteenth century, when a diamond ring was placed onto the fourth finger of the left hand because that finger was believed to carry the vein of love that continued directly to the heart. A diamond engagement ring is still a luxurious demonstration of love, no matter what size it is. My tiny diamond ring was given to me with the same amount of love as the ring Prince William gave to Kate Middleton and, irrespective of its cost, my ring meant just as much to me as hers did to her.

Whether we earn a lot or a little, the choices are the same. 'Where your treasure is, there your heart will be also' (Matt. 6:21). We don't need to wait to share our homes, to share a word of praise, to give a gift or to serve at church until we feel we have all of our own needs met (we never will), and we don't need to store up more treasures than we will ever use. We can choose instead to elevate the dreams and needs of others and play an exciting part by encouraging them and seeing them flourish.

I know a lady who leaks lavish love. She is like a whirlwind of blessing who deposits gifts, meals, invitations and encouraging notes wherever she goes. She is also one of the busiest people I have ever met, with an extremely demanding occupation. I suspect that she gets enormous pleasure from building up other people and seeing them delighted and supported in what they are doing, and I thank God for her. I also owe a debt of gratitude to the faithful friends who allow me to blather on about my frustrations and failures and then encourage me to stand taller and walk further than I ever have before. Some people will generously sacrifice their time and willingly give us precious gifts of wisdom, attention and prayer. What priceless treasures they are.

You might not have spare pounds in your purse, but you may have the ability to babysit or to pick up some ironing or shopping. You might not be great with words, but you could well be the owner of a very warm hug. God is asking you to be lavish. To share the diamonds you do have. He longs for you to give yourself wholeheartedly in worship and to saturate yourself in his presence and his word. He is urging you to generously and liberally bless others in whatever ways you can. He asks you to arrange and prioritise your own resources so that you can create a model of living that frees you to grow in a deeper knowledge of God's provision and pleasure in your life.

And as we pour out, he keeps pouring out in abundance. As we are lavish in love, we witness the blessing of our limitless God, who touches the world through the hands of his people.

That's something we all want more of. Wouldn't you agree?

DIGGING DEEPER

- Have you ever given or received a diamond? What gifts have you received that have felt the most heartfelt or lavish to you? Why were they so special?

- Have you ever been blessed by somebody who was not materially rich but who was extraordinarily generous in their own way? How did they do that?

- How infected do you think you are with the bug of wanting more?

- How aware and disciplined are you about your earning, spending, saving and giving? Would a budget help? Do you see this process as being spiritual?

- Do you find it easier to spend or to save? What could you learn about balancing these two?

- How could you adopt a simpler lifestyle to leave more room for generous living?

- Does anything ever get in the way of you worshipping God wholeheartedly? How can you overcome these things?

- Think about your home, your money, your time, your words and your gifts. How could you become more lavish in your love for others?

Lavish and loving God,

I thank you that your word tells me that you supply all of my needs according to your riches in glory. You never hold back. I also thank you for every generous act and every sacrifice made that has blessed me. I pray, Lord God, that you would increase my gratitude and my dependence upon you. You are more than enough for me. Help me to resist the constant pull to fill my soul with more of what I don't need and to look to you to pour into me the love that I do need. Lord, let my worship of you be wholehearted and true. And may my love for others be as extravagant and lavish as you have been to me.

In the name of Jesus, who gave everything for me,

Amen

PURPOSE

Chapter 10

INHERITED

> But the plans of the Lord stand firm for ever,
> the purposes of his heart through all generations.
> Blessed is the nation whose God is the Lord,
> the people he chose for his inheritance.
>
> Psalm 33:11–12

One of my favourite series on the goggle-box is *Who Do You Think You Are?* where each week a familiar famous face traces their heritage and discovers that they are, in fact, related to wartime heroes, kings, workhouse fodder or maniacal axe-murderers. It's compulsive viewing. I have always been partial to a bit of genealogy, and remember talking for hours with a distant relative who, before the days of the Internet, had researched our family tree back to 1734, discovering a long-lost relative called Cissy Inkpen, a family lion tamer, some miners, and a smattering of dubious parentage. More recently, however, it has been suggested that our family lineage can be traced right back to Cleopatra. How marvellous!

Finally I have an explanation for my longstanding addiction to lashings of black eyeliner, my love of a good bath and my ability to get through gallons of milk (albeit not usually together).

Most of us find it mind-boggling to consider that we exist at the end of a long line of ancestors, most of whom we know nothing about. In turn, it is equally humbling to realise that each of us will one day be simply a name in history for the grandchildren of our grandchildren. But what will our legacy be? What are the things of value that you and I have received that we want to pass on? Will there be things apart from my eye colour and my shoes that are handed down through the generations? (They will keep my shoes, right?)

A Precious Legacy

I don't come from a wealthy family with large inheritances, but I already have a few precious possessions from my nan and from my grandma, who is still alive but currently distributing her belongings like sweets amongst the family. Upon my pine dresser are numerous items of cheery blue and white striped Cornishware crockery, which she was originally given a piece at a time by her mother each time she came to visit from Wales. And I am also the current custodian of the beautiful ruby and diamond necklace that my grandpa bought for my grandma to celebrate their ruby wedding anniversary. It's not an enormous jewel or a spectacularly pricey pendant, but it doesn't matter. I count it a real privilege to now be the steward of each of these pieces of their life together.

INHERITED

But long before my grandparents started to dispense with the treasures in their cupboards, my grandma and grandpa would share other pearls of wisdom with us. After a musical afternoon playing the piano, the banjo or the accordion, while chomping on tuna sarnies and trifle we would revel in the tales of bicycle rides over the Welsh mountains or wartime stories, including the rescue of the piano from the bombing, and we would often pick up on phrases that have become part of the fabric of our lives. I particularly love the James M. Barrie quote 'God gave us memory so that we might have June roses in December.' that my grandma would say every time we shared a lovely day or a special event: 'God gave us memory so that we might have June roses in December.'[9]

Even today she will remind me that I am collecting June roses whenever we share our holiday photographs with her. Whilst we might have a million digital images and Facebook updates to help us recall the chronology of our lives, our memory is still our most powerful collector of significant moments and emotions. All of us are receiving an inheritance of ideas and impressions into our lives from the parents, teachers, friends, mentors, church leaders, spouses or grandparents who have deposited gems into our lives, and they form an important part of who we become.

I think it is fair to say that at school I was not exactly the popular kid. Firstly, I looked like a boy. For some inexplicable

[9] J.M. Barrie, from the rectorial address he delivered to the Red Gowns at St Andrew's University, Canada, 3 May 1922

reason Mum allowed the hairdresser to chop my hair shorter than your average Royal Marine, until I was about 15 years old and rebelled. Also, I needed eight teeth removed, had countless braces and was blessed with a figure like a skinny Twiglet that was then engulfed in a giant duffle coat of humiliation. If that were not bad enough, every day I rode to school on a brown bicycle that was commonly known by others as 'the tank'. It did indeed weigh the same as a small armoured vehicle and as it advanced slowly forwards on its tiny white but offensively wide wheels, it achieved its mission of denying me any social acceptance amongst my BMX-riding peers. I am sure my parents meant well, but really . . .

Despite my lack of street cred, there were some folk at my tatty comprehensive school who made me feel really special. They were my teachers. In particular, my home from home every day was the music department. I knew that every time I stepped into that classroom, I was amongst my people. We might have been an odd tribe (not every 14-year-old gets excited about an oboe solo) but we were united together in our weirdness. My music teacher was, without a doubt, one of the most influential adults in my life. When he saw me, he saw potential. He gave me his time, laughed with me, shared events with me, worked with me to improve my skills and he cared about me – and many other pupils besides me. When I married Mark, a few years later, my music teacher came to the wedding with some of his other pupils and performed a song that he had composed especially for that day.

That wonderful legacy continues. As I help my children with preparation for their music theory exams or as

I watch them play in their school jazz band with their own dedicated and enthusiastic teachers I am deeply aware that some of their experiences are an inheritance received directly from the musical home of my grandparents, the time and money of my parents and the commitment and passion of my own music teachers.

A Deliberate Investment

For most of us, however, while we have much to be thankful for, not everything we have received has been a blessing. Some of the experiences and influences that have colonised our minds have been unhelpful or even painful. The question is, will we reproduce and pass down those same traits and mistakes or can we, with God's help and perhaps a great counsellor or friend, halt the flow and replace it with something more positive? We do not have to repeat the past, where it is damaging. We can, with God's help, create a different future and a healthier heritage.

Once we realise that we all reproduce ourselves in some way and create a culture around us, so we can deliberately continue to surrender who we are to God and seek to grow in Christ-likeness and maturity, so that the habits, the values and the passions that we replicate are as fruitful and healthy as possible.

As a parent, I have often been encouraged and challenged by the proverb in the Bible that says, 'Train up a child in the way he should go; even when he is old he will not depart from it' (Prov. 22:6, ESV). What I wouldn't give for a cast-iron money-back guarantee which reassures me that as I pour the right stuff into my children's lives they will be sure to follow a good and godly, positive and pain-free life for the rest of their days. Sadly, such a thing does not exist. However, the principle in this proverb remains true. As we consciously invest in the lives of others – whether that is our own children, the young people around us, younger Christians or even friends whom we support – what we invest will often reproduce itself over and over again.

The call of discipleship is to be people of faith who reproduce God's values. Jesus' last words to his followers were to go and make disciples. To pour out into others all that God has invested into us. We are to deliberately share our faith and also encourage people to grow into maturity and ministry. I suspect, however, that many of us fall into the trap of believing we have nothing of real value to share. We might feel that there must be hundreds of people more qualified, more mature and more together than we are to pass on faith and to do the Lord's work. But all of us have something we can pass on to somebody else and all of us are needed in God's plans. If we are married, we can help a younger married couple. If we are single, we can share life with and support somebody else who is on their own and be an incredible aunty or uncle figure. If we are in business, we can mentor a graduate. If we have been a Christian for more than a month, then we can share the journey with somebody who has been a Christian for less than a month!

> But all of us have something we can pass on to somebody else and all of us are needed in God's plans.

There is a desperate need for more accountable and purposeful relationships in the church and in our communities. When I see women, still stumbling over their identity and doubting their value, preoccupied with their weight or their looks, I want to stand alongside them in the same way that other women have stood with me over the years. I can't claim to be a highly trained mentor, but I can reassure a young mum that toddler tantrums do pass and help another person to appreciate and develop their talents. I can, at the very least, offer to eat cake, ask questions, listen and pray. Not surprisingly, it is often as we simply give God the chance to enter a conversation with a friend that our thoughts and plans begin to distil in ways we had never expected.

The Generation Game

It is wonderful to think that you have the opportunity to intentionally model and pass on what you consider to be valuable to those around you. Some of these treasures will have been gained through positive and exciting experiences, and some you will have found the hard way, through life lessons that you can now share with others. But either way, God has given you treasure which somebody else can benefit from.

Those of us who are parents or who are responsible for children have an especially significant task. We are in a privileged position (yes – even you who haven't slept for more than five hours in the last week!), and as we sit back for a moment and look past our taxi-driving, money-giving, uniform-ironing, homework-hustling lives, we might be able to imagine the future for families and for the church in this country, and indeed across the world. We have a particular and pressing responsibility to invest in this generation who will face so many challenges and who, statistically speaking, are less likely than ever to keep their faith into their adult years. God is asking us to build homes and families of love and faith.

> These commandments that I give you today are to be on your hearts. Impress them on your children. Talk about them when you sit at home and when you walk along the road, when you lie down and when you get up. Tie them as symbols on your hands and bind them on your foreheads. Write them on the door-frames of your houses and on your gates.
>
> Deuteronomy 6:6–9

As parents, the most significant thing we could ever do is to model a genuine and honest faith to our children and to equip them to be globally minded, compassionate, committed individuals who will, we hope, change the world as they serve God wherever they are. It is not the sole responsibility of their youth workers or their teachers to show them how to be a disciple, how to care for the poor or to challenge and develop their aspirations, although they are critically important role models who deserve our support and encouragement. Children are like human sponges, absorbing every drop of their environment; their young minds are shaped by the impressions

Children are like human sponges, absorbing every drop of their environment.

and discussions around them. And so, be in no doubt, our conversations around the dinner table, the way we welcome people into our homes, the tone in which we speak to them and about others, as well as the choices we make with our time and money will all influence their values and priorities, perhaps more than we care to realise.

But it's not just about parenting. I remember we once had somebody come to speak to our church about how we engage with younger people around us. She made some excellent points and I nodded enthusiastically in agreement with her, as you do. And then after the service I found myself talking to a friend with her teenage daughter standing beside her. I realised to my shame, that I had not even acknowledged her presence and probably had rarely done so before. I stopped in my tracks. I turned to this beautiful and talented young person and asked how school was going. It was as if somebody had turned a switch on and she lit up as she was included and valued. I will admit that I felt extremely rebuked at how I had unintentionally made her feel. Since that day, I have enjoyed deliberately engaging with some vibrant and sometimes chaotic young people, both at our church and through the friendships of our girls. I sometimes cringe at their conversation, and I often laugh helplessly at their antics, but we are blessed to know them and if they have chosen to worship God over staying in bed or hanging out at the park with their mates, then they deserve our encouragement.

Of course, none of us are perfect role models and there is not a parent, a youth worker or a children's volunteer who has not made some mistakes. Personally, there are many moments that I wish I could rewind and try again. Wouldn't that be a great facility to have? But there are plenty of wonderful parents and leaders out there who have done so much right and still had their hearts broken by seeing children make choices they would never have made for them. In fact, even God, the perfect Father, had to watch Adam and Eve making some very bad decisions. But we must not be discouraged and we must never underestimate or take for granted the God-given influence we have upon the lives of our young people. And, more than anything, we must pray for them.

Protect or Neglect

Our faith and our values are incredibly precious. The Bible tells us that there is a thief who would steal and destroy our faith and, like a jewel, if we want to pass it on, it needs protection.

I remember reading about a spectacular heist that took place halfway through the great exhibition in the London Millennium Dome in 2000. A gang of men planned to break in and steal the twelve incredibly valuable diamonds that were being exhibited, including the Millennium Star – a whopping 203-carat near-perfect jewel. Altogether these stones had an estimated value of more than £350 million. The robbers successfully forced their way through the fencing and entrance with a mechanical digger while a fast getaway boat lay in wait on the Thames nearby. However, the police were aware of the plans. The evening before, the diamonds had been replaced by dummy crystal replicas, and when the robbers burst into the so-called

INHERITED

Money Zone the police were ready to arrest them all, along with the crew of the boat.

There is a conspiracy to rob us of what we hold dear, and our faith is under fire. Around the world today Christians are being actively persecuted for their beliefs. Closer to home, our values are being eroded, undermined and usurped by other idols, and the church is in danger of drifting blissfully into irrelevance. It is time for us to protect and insure our faith against loss – to be more prepared and purposeful than ever before about protecting the precious inheritance God has given us and about actively pursuing what we believe. We may declare and pray that the next generation will take the jewels of faith that we pass on to them and go faster and further than we have ever gone, but if that faith becomes diluted and weak in our possession, it will be much harder for us to pass the baton on to those coming after us.

In our digitally connected and well-informed world, we are more than able to take part in the discussion about social issues and legislation and to petition where needed. We can also easily support and encourage those who are standing up for their beliefs in demanding arenas. In our own schools, homes and workplaces we can actively engage and reaffirm the godly values that build strong communities. And for the future of our church we need to strap on our seatbelts and sacrifice generously, serve outrageously and pursue relentlessly the mission of God in our generation. It is our calling to be devoted and countercultural believers ourselves, in order to nurture and make other culture-changing disciples. Nobody else is going to do it for us. It is our great commission and our time is now.

A Spiritual Inheritance

When we moved to Locks Heath, more than a decade ago, we unexpectedly spent a few months living with a couple from our new church who really understand what it means to pass on all that God has given them. Our two children were very young, our house sale had fallen through again and again, and I remember feeling very unsure about sharing our family chaos with people I hardly knew. Viv and Maggie, however, understood then, as they do now, that God has given them everything they need and the wherewithal to invest it in others. Most of their married life, somebody has been living alongside them in their home. Half of our church leadership team is comprised of people who grew up and found faith in a youth group held in their front room, in the years when their own children were young. Now, in their retirement they are still visiting people, welcoming people and dis-playing an uncanny ability to laugh outrageously, to care deeply and to challenge when it is needed. Their legacy, which continues to grow, is evidence of the treasure that they have discovered in Christ and their commitment to passing it on.

You see, while we expect to inherit physical features, strengths and aspirations from our biological family, we are also a part of a spiritual family with a spiritual inheritance. We are, as Christians, adopted into God's family and therefore connected to an incredible line of ancestors – Abraham, King David and even Jesus. We might not be linked genetically, but spiritually there is no doubt that we are. As we surrender our lives to God through Jesus, we become a vital part of a family of believers who have passed down the faith from generation to generation. What is more, our adoption into God's family is absolute and incorruptible, stronger than a legal document, purer than blood and founded in unconditional love. Romans 8:15–17 (NLT) tells us, 'You received God's Spirit when he adopted you as his own children. Now we call him, "Abba, Father." For his Spirit joins with our spirit to affirm that we are God's children. And since we are his children, we are his heirs.'

This means we have a spiritual inheritance that is guaranteed to be ours. But I do not believe this means that every promise made to an individual in the Bible or every blessing bestowed upon anybody in Scripture is now our personal entitlement and ours for the taking. While it is undeniably true that most of us have barely scratched the surface of all that God wants to do in our lives, our inheritance is so much more than simply getting our own way or being guaranteed a healthy and wealthy life. In fact, Romans 8 continues: 'And since we are his children, we are his heirs. In fact, together with Christ we are heirs of God's glory. But if we are to share his glory, we must also share his suffering. Yet what we suffer now is nothing compared to the glory he will reveal to us later' (vv.17–18).

No father promises his children that every path ahead will always be easy. Life just isn't like that. But our Heavenly Father reassures us that as followers of and co-heirs with

Christ, he is giving us the ultimate treasures of his presence, his purpose and his peace, now and forever. He has given to us untold and glorious riches through the Spirit and in his word, and we have the privilege of being able to mine those treasures with him.

Every Sunday I am reminded that I am a citizen of heaven with a spiritual family. I love it when we sing the words from the wonderful hymn 'Be Thou My Vision' that say, 'You my inheritance, now and always'. Our Father is the High King of heaven and as we sing these words and declare together Jesus' prayer, 'Your kingdom come, your will be done, on earth as it is in heaven,' we are choosing to live with an awareness of God's reign in our life and to accept our role in bringing about his purposes in our lifetime.

The good news is that wherever God calls us, he will always equip us and walk with us, his children. We can rest in the knowledge that we are not alone or dependent upon our own efforts or limited perspective. The question is, will we truly live in the light of the resources and the inheritance God has given us? We must own for ourselves all God has given to us in order

God is passing us the baton. He has given us some precious heirlooms to protect and to pass on.

to share these riches with another generation of believers. Our inheritance is never only for our benefit, just as our family tree doesn't end with us. God asks us to pass the blessings of faith, hope and love down to the future generations.

INHERITED

God is passing us the baton. He has given us some precious heirlooms to protect and to pass on. We are not here to simply store up treasures for ourselves. As Matthew 6 tells us, we are called to store our treasures in heaven, our heavenly home, and to leave a legacy that will last far beyond our own years. That is a precious inheritance.

DIGGING DEEPER

- Do you own a piece of jewellery or another item that you have inherited? How do you feel about it knowing it was passed down to you?

- Are there other traditions, sayings or traits that are a part of your inheritance?

- Who are the key people who have most significantly invested in your life? Why did they make such an impact?

- How are you involved in mentoring or encouraging others? Is there more you could do?

- How can you more intentionally pass on your faith and values to the next generation? Could you also encourage others who are working to support children and young people?

- What are the main ways you can protect and safeguard your own faith and the legacy of our faith in our society?

- What does it mean for you to live in awareness of the spiritual inheritance God has given to you?

178

Heavenly Father,

I thank you that you have given me a spiritual family and a heavenly inheritance. You are a wonderful Heavenly Father and I thank you for the great riches of your presence, your word and your peace. Lord, I pray for the next generation, who you love, and I ask that my generation will pass on the baton to them so that they can build strong relationships, grow deep in faith and shape their world. Help me, Lord, to invest in others with whatever I have been given and to trust in you.

Amen

Chapter 11

MULTIFACETED

The ways of right-living people glow with light; the longer they live, the brighter they shine.

Proverbs 4:18, MSG

You've probably heard the well-known saying that 'many hands make light work'. Well, I'm sure that's true, but my experience of life suggests that quite often it's more likely to be 'two hands juggle way too much work'. I must be getting something wrong somewhere. Am I just terrible at asking for help? (Answer: yes.) Am I prone to taking on way too much to start with? (Answer: definitely.) Do I secretly think that half the time it is quicker and easier to just do things myself rather than grunt at people if they do it wrong? (Guilty, m' Lord.) But I don't think I am alone, and I don't think it's just my control-freakery either. The pace of life just seems to get faster and faster.

Scientists tell us that we process more pieces of information a day than at any time in history – five times more than we did even in the mid-eighties.[10] It's possible, and normal now, for us to correspond with people hourly as opposed to monthly. In fact, through social media we can get a response from almost any company instantaneously. With the wizardry of my smartphone I can find pretty much any information about anything at any time of the day, and if I want to learn how to make a skirt or how to fix the car, I can just browse the Internet for instructions and off I go. In order to keep on top of my diverse portfolio of daily activities, I can bring up my fabulously colour-coded digital diary so that I can see different clients, responsibilities and family events clearly and quickly and get reminders sent to me so that I get to the right place at the right time with the right information while simultaneously doing the grocery shopping online. I can, apparently, be a professional, a writer, a volunteer, a mum, a chef, a taxi driver, a counsellor, a wife, a friend, an event planner, financial administrator and a home-builder all at the same time, and sparkle all the way.

Sure I can.

I mean, is it all ever really possible? Can we really have it all and at the same time? For most people I know, the to-do list never gets any shorter, even if it is brilliantly updated across all the digital platforms. And no matter how many plates I manage to keep spinning, it seems to me that there is always some other mega-faceted person who seems to manage even more than I do and still look instagramazing at the same time.

[10]www.telegraph.co.uk/science/science-news/8316534/Welcome-to-the-information-age-174-newspapers-a-day.html

So how do I respond to this conundrum? Quite often with guilt, if I am honest. There have been times when I have felt that I should somehow just be better, try harder, be nicer and pray longer. But this is, to put it mildly, unproductive. Guilt is never a good master and the pressure of others should never define us or be our motivation, no matter how compelling the case we are presented with. The reality is that we are supposed to be multifaceted people who live diverse and interesting lives, with various roles and responsibilities. But there is a limit. The question is, how do we endure the whirl of activity, ensuring that we still define ourselves and face the right direction at the right time, in a way that brings light, life and beauty?

Light Fantastic

Of all the things I have learned about diamonds through the writing of this book, the thing that has captivated me most is the unique way they play with light. Light travels at 186,000 miles per second, but slows when it travels through matter such as glass, air or water. However, when it travels through a diamond, light does something amazing – it slows down to half its normal speed. The atoms in a diamond are so densely packed that it completely changes the way that light travels.

And although light will enter a diamond from every side, it will bounce around inside until it finds a clean and straight exit route back out again. The greater the distance this light travels inside the diamond, the more the white light reveals the rainbow of colours contained inside. This is because as the light bounces around, the colours separate or disperse, creating a prism light show. Other gemstones can disperse white light to a point, but none come close to a diamond's ability to disperse a rainbow of colour in different directions. It is known as the diamond's 'fire'.

It is incredible to think that a diamond can change how light travels: that it can slow it down, bend it, disperse it, reveal the colours in it and ultimately let it shine out in a dazzling display. So, it is vital that each diamond is cut to maximise its unique brilliance (the way it reflects and refracts light). Whether it is the ubiquitous round 'brilliant' cut with 58 facets or the popular 'emerald' or 'princess' cuts, each diamond has been fastidiously angled and shaped to enhance the light shining through it.

But here's the thing: there comes a point when more facets simply would not contribute any further to the cut of the diamond. The light has been maximised. In fact, adding more facets would change the character of the gem and actually deaden the fire.

Which leads me to consider whether we are guilty of trying to cut more facets into our life than we could ever shine light through. Is it possible that we are actually deadening the fire inside us by trying to add more sparkle? Would God be able to shine more brightly and more brilliantly in certain directions through us if we weren't trying to spread what we have so thinly?

> Is it possible that we are actually deadening the fire inside us by trying to add more sparkle?

MULTIFACETED

Have you ever had the chance to watch a drummer playing a drum kit with skill and flair? While at school, I spent a few years learning to bash the drums, but never really mastered the art of persuading my four limbs to each play something different simultaneously. So I watch the drummers I know with some serious admiration. Can you imagine being able to play one rhythm with one hand, another pattern with the other and then to play two other completely different arrangements with your feet – but all together, in a way that sounds cohesive? But the magic really begins to happen when, after lots of practice and adding those parts individually, the drummer somehow stops consciously thinking and plays it automatically, allowing the music to flow through until the rhythms all blend into one, allowing them the freedom to play and adapt it as they play. It's a pretty remarkable thing.

We are designed to be multi-dimensional people and to 'play different rhythms' at the same time. It is as if our lives are able to beat out a single rhythm that is constructed from a complex polyphony of parts. We are made up of the different facets of our responsibility and personality and the beauty occurs when, instead of each element disrupting each other, we allow the grace of God to pour through us into all we do until we find the delicate balance and the freedom to play and adapt.

But do you know what? If while our imaginary drummer was in full flow you threw him a violin and asked him to integrate it into his music, it would be a disaster. He couldn't do it. He doesn't have the fingers spare or the skill or passion for it. It's one thing too many. And yet

I can't tell you how many times somebody has thrown me something that is neither within my capability nor my capacity and yet I have felt compelled to 'drop my drumsticks' and try anyway. This is a sign of great silliness on my part.

Perhaps one of the advantages of growing slightly older is finally understanding that while we are called to do many things with enthusiasm and passion, none of us can do everything, and nor should we.

Setting Matters

Every precious stone, with its many facets, needs a setting in order to sparkle most effectively. They are not really fit for a purpose until they are placed in gold or hung on a chain. You can't really see the light properly bounce through them until they are placed in such a way as to maximise their unique qualities. And just as diamonds are placed in royal crowns to create a display of grandeur and awe, so we will shine forth the glory of God and his faithful and loving care for his people as we display his goodness and mercy. As Zechariah 9:16 so beautifully says, 'The Lord their God will save his people on that day as a shepherd saves his flock. They will sparkle in his land like jewels in a crown.'

Where we are placed matters. I love finding the right setting for people. In fact, I like to think of myself as a bit of a one-woman HR department. There is nothing more rewarding to me than finding exactly the right place for people to shine. I get genuinely excited about seeing fellow followers using their gifts and skills in their career and in the church in a way that brings life to them and light to others. When we find a place where we are a round peg in a round hole we thrive and reflect an important element of colour from the spectrum of God's love. Jesus tells us in Luke 11, that our light should not be hidden under a bowl, it should be set on a stand for people to see. Our faith, together with our talents, our skills and our compassion, should radiate in a confident and visible demonstration of his love towards his world, and he needs us to find our place and stand in it.

I won't ever be a great artist or a wonderful counsellor, but when I am given the opportunity to communicate, to imagine or to lead, I know I am in a setting that magnifies and intensifies the light God has placed in me. Likewise, when I am in the wrong place, I just feel frustrated and impatient. I probably whine more than shine.

I remember when I was once (and only once) asked to serve tea and coffee at church. I was torn – because you know you ought to say yes, but to be honest the enthusiasm wasn't really forthcoming. But, trying to be helpful, I smiled weakly and mumbled, 'Yes of course!' I went into the kitchen only to be greeted by the biggest mother of a stainless steel teapot I have ever seen. Who makes these giant teapots? How huge are their biceps? Anyway, before I knew it there were two ladies leading the orderly queue that was forming. I was already breaking out into beads of nervous sweat when one of them said to me, 'Hello dear, I'll have a tea please. Make it nice and strong though.'

Her friend then added, 'Oh yes, I'll have tea too, love, but I like mine weak.'

I looked at them. I looked at the overgrown teapot. And I said, 'Do I look like a magician to you ladies?'

As they stood and pondered my ineptitude, I stood there silently asking myself how to perform a miracle with one pot containing a random quantity of fairly traded tea bags. And what's the issue anyway? I mean it's not like a steak that you want medium-rare or whatever, is it? It's tea!

Like I said. Only asked once.

In retrospect, I probably should have had the confidence to say that the kitchen was not my ideal setting – although sometimes all of us have to step out and serve out of our comfort zones, and I appreciate those people who serve the tea a whole lot more now. (By the way, you apparently dilute the tea with hot water in the cup. Who knew?)

At other times, God leads us and places us into a new setting which takes a while to settle into. I will confess that becoming a wife and a mother early in my twenties took some adjustment. Like many women, I had previously formed an identity as a student, a friend and a colleague, but suddenly my *raison d'être* had been turned upside down. I found myself as a new mum wobbling and hurting in places I didn't know I had places, and swimming in baby wipes and sterilising fluid whilst staring at a screaming and wriggling bundle that apparently had no off switch. It seemed unfair that neither of the kids came with an instruction manual. And even being married was what I would politely call a 'learning curve'. I felt marooned and found myself saying to people that I was 'just' a mum (which is as oxymoronic as you could ever be), until I more fully embraced the privilege and calling it is to share my life with these crazy, wonderful people.

Shine Like Stars

We may not always be in a position to choose the perfect job or the ideal situation for ourselves, and sometimes it takes a while to get used to a setting that we really love, but we can make a choice to be positive and to shine where God has placed us. And there may be a setting that gets our heart racing with excitement closer than we realise. It takes a leap of faith to go self-employed, to go on a mission trip or to join a new area of work or ministry, but sometimes that might be what it takes. It requires some vulnerability to invest in new friendships, to join a new network or to get involved in a cause. But we know that when we begin setting ourselves apart and stepping out in a way that gives God pleasure, we will see his light shine through us far more than when we tried to stay safe in order to avoid the risk of failure or rejection.

This matters, because you and I are designed to reflect the light. Throughout the Bible, God has been using light as a metaphor for his goodness that radiates throughout the earth. From the moment in Genesis when God says 'Let there be light' until the final chapter of Revelation, when we hear that the people of God 'will not need the light of a lamp or the light of the sun, for the Lord God will give them light' (Rev. 22:5), there is a clear sense that the Lord is our light and his word and his presence are a lamp to our feet that illuminates our way (Ps. 119:105).

It's important that we grab hold of the fact that we ourselves are not the light. Our own efforts and good intentions are not the answer to the needs of the world, so much as a conduit through which we direct the light of God as he shines through us. John, at the beginning of his Gospel, clarifies this, explaining that he himself is not the light but a witness to Jesus, the Light of the World. He also tells us, 'In him was life, and that life was the light of all mankind. The light shines in the darkness, and the darkness has not overcome it' (John 1:4–5).

We, his people, are called to make a difference to the darkness, as God chooses to shine his light through us. And just as a pure diamond reflects visible light, but also ultraviolet light and infrared light and all the frequencies in between, God will work in us and through us both in ways we will see and also in a myriad of ways we will be totally unaware of but which will banish darkness and bless the world. Therefore, just as every facet of a diamond has the potential to alter a light's plane of travel, so each facet of our life must also be considered to see whether the path of God's light is being disrupted or enhanced through it. Are we, in short, bouncing the light or deadening the fire?

I clearly remember sitting in the car one day with the children when my youngest daughter innocently asked me whether I was going to be a better grandparent than I was a parent. Kids are great like that, aren't they? Really. Great. After I had finished sobbing into the steering wheel I asked her what she meant, since I spent half of my life on mumsy duties. 'Well,' she replied, 'it's just that you're always busy and you don't really do much fun stuff.'

The awkward thing is that she was right. Despite the fact that I would say to anybody that my children are the most precious part of my life, the reality was that I was not radiating any joy or light into their lives at that time. I was coping with a thousand responsibilities that I felt all required my focus and attention, leaving me dim and drained for the people I cared about most.

So if I asked you, as I ask myself again today, what the top priority is that God has given you at the moment, would you be able to tell me? Where is he asking you to shine his love primarily? What about numbers two and three? How much of your time and attention is spent focused upon those areas where he has asked you to direct his light and how much of your time is spent on nothing to do with things that really matter to you? Every now and then I like to sit down and prayerfully review my calendar, and promptly panic. But instead of getting caught up in the spiral of doom and gloom, complaining about having to do so many things (that I quite possibly shouldn't be doing), I challenge myself to focus more on what God *has* told me to do and to shine brighter in those places. And if other things need to go then, as hard as that is, I will have to let them go. As Paul reminds us:

> Do everything without grumbling or arguing, so that you may become blameless and pure, 'children of God without fault in a warped and crooked generation.' Then you

will shine among them like stars in the sky as you hold firmly to the word of life.

Philippians 2:14–16

Wherever we are and whatever stage of life we are currently navigating, just as a diamond needs to be placed at an angle towards the light in order to sparkle, so we need to make sure we are orientated towards God to shine like stars in a dark sky. If we want his light to shine through us, then we need to go back to the source of the light and spend time in his presence. His goodness is the light that we so desperately need, and in both our times of busyness and our times of stillness, as we turn to face our maker, we know for sure that he, and the full technicolour spectrum of his love, is also turned towards us.

As strange and extraordinary as it seems, the Light of the World has given you and me the ability to disperse his glorious love and to show others just how brightly he shines. Every God-given facet of our life has the potential to be a revelation of his love to a world covered in darkness.

So, go ahead. Permission to sparkle.

DIGGING DEEPER

- Thinking of how diamonds reflect, refract and disperse light, what do you think are the barriers to the light shining through effectively? Does this teach you anything?

- Thinking of your multifaceted life, are there too many areas fighting for your attention right now or are you able to balance your roles and responsibilities well? Is there anything you should be putting down?

- How do you respond when asked to take on more than you are able to cope with? Why?

- Would you say you are in an ideal setting to shine at the moment or not? How can you maximise your position or even find a new setting?

- What would you say are your top three priorities at the moment? Are you able to give them the time and attention they need? What other stuff gets in the way?

- What are the most helpful ways for you to face the light of God? How do you best discover his presence and power?

- How can you regularly remember to pray that God will shine through you, wherever you are? Is there a visual reminder that could prompt you?

Lord Jesus,

I thank you that you are the Light of the World, and that there is no darkness found in you. Lord, teach me to discern why I do what I do, and help me to do no more and no less than you ask of me. I give you again the things that are most precious in my life and ask that you would use me to shine your love, your forgiveness, your justice and your hope into the places you have called me to. Lord, I pray that you would let there be light in the darkness of this world, and that you would use me to shine brightly in every facet of my life.

For your glory, I pray,

Amen

Chapter 12

TRANSFORMED

And we all, who with unveiled faces contemplate the Lord's glory, are being transformed into his image with ever-increasing glory, which comes from the Lord, who is the Spirit.

2 Corinthians 3:18

I'm not renowned for my scientific knowledge. My physics-loving daughter is constantly astonished at my lack of awareness of how newtons work and my ambivalence about the wonders of quantum mechanics. So, perhaps it is no surprise that I am still baffled and amazed that diamonds are, at the end of the day, just common old carbon. When I throw a bucket of dirty coal onto my fire, I'm also looking at carbon. It's the same stuff. It seems incredible to me that left for the right amount of time under the right conditions, that dark and messy substance is completely transformed into something we treasure so highly.

It is equally baffling to me that as I look at the raw and messy material of my own life, God can take it and transform it in the same way. Just as carbon can be changed from something that is burned and discarded into something that is treasured and displayed proudly, so God desires for you and me to be changed and renewed too. Now that is astonishing.

Of course, being a woman I know all about transform-ation. From the moment of waking until I leave the house, a significant metamorphic process takes place. By the time I have straightened, concealed, plucked and shaped, I am almost unrecognisable. And praise the Lord for that! But a woman's work is never done, and when I recently visited a local department store, I was accosted by a gorgeous young saleswoman with a dangly name badge saying, 'Steph – Can I help you?' Steph clearly felt that my face still needed some help.

'Have you seen our world-renowned patented-tech-nology eyeliner?' she asked me. 'It is, no word of a lie, completely revolutionary. Once you have tried this product I promise you will wonder how you ever lived without it.'

Bold claim for an eyeliner. I was impressed and paused a fraction too long.

'Sit down,' Steph instructed me in a tone which implied I had little choice in the matter. 'Let's get this on you and change your life once and for all.'

Righto then.

'First of all,' said Steph, now in full flow, prodding my skin and shaking her head with concern as I sat as her captive, 'I think we need to apply some of our famous face-primer.'

That's right. Primer. I use primer on my woodwork and my walls and, okay, I accept my face has some surface cracks forming, but really? Still, I sat until I was suitably primed.

'Now, before we apply our patented and award-winning eyeliner, I think it might be a good idea to just frame your eyes with our unique 3-dimensional textured and fibred eyebrow product.'

Steph brandished her weapon, assumed the posture, and I didn't even bother to respond. She set to work, sculpting my brows with the aid of said 3-dimensional eyebrow product and then added the life-changing eyeliner. After a few minutes, she stood back and regarded her masterpiece as Van Gogh must have regarded his sunflowers.

'You are not going to believe this. You are transformed!' she exclaimed, handing me a mirror. 'Are you ready for this?'

I was transformed alright. Into a drag queen. My eyebrows were so full of personality they could have hosted their own chat show. 'Crikey!' I spluttered. 'They certainly are a . . . '

'I know,' interrupted Steph, 'they're a real feature now, aren't they! Now, which of these ground-breaking products are you going to take home with you today?'

And because I am British, I told Steph that she really has a special talent and I must of course buy the wretched eyeliner and the crack-filling primer, and that I was deeply grateful for the opportunity of doing so.

So is this the only transformation that I can hope for? Filled cracks and legendary eyebrows? When God looks at me, is that what he is concerned about transforming? Thankfully, I think he is interested in something far more significant than my ageing features.

Dig for Victory

A couple of years ago I think God wanted to teach me a few more important lessons about what real transformation looks like. Much to the amusement of my husband, I signed up for an allotment. I had been on the waiting list for a while, and finally my time came. I was the proud owner of an enormous plot of weeds. The thing is, in my mind I had delightful images of me wafting through beanstalks and picking berries to put into my wicker baskets and my floral bags. I had painted a full-scale *Country Living* idyll in my imagination – of sunny deckchair days and friendly chats across wheelbarrows. I had completely lost the vegetable plot.

> We are all motivated when we have a clear and compelling idea of what the final goal is.

It turns out that transformation is jolly hard work. Before you even get around to planting anything, you have to remove all of the damaging roots, dig out the rocks and create healthy spaces in which to plant your carefully chosen seeds. This is what the experts call back-breaking work. I am ashamed to admit that I became totally discouraged after a few months and passed the allotment on to my friend, who came along cheerily with tools, salvaged useful items and had a clear idea of what that plot could be. She is now the one enjoying bountiful harvests of courgettes and an endless supply of twenty types of tomatoes, and she also has the satisfaction of knowing that she has transformed that piece of waste ground into a healthy and productive plot.

The vital thing that was missing for me as I worked that ground was a clear picture of what I was aiming at. I got waylaid by the weeds and exasperated by the rocks and, as a result, I lost sight of what that piece of ground was all about. We are all motivated when we have a clear and compelling idea of what the final goal is. Otherwise, the digging just feels hard. Whether we are fixing somebody's face, digging an allotment, making a cake or starting a business, our vision of what we are creating is always our most motivating factor.

God is completely committed to our transformation. But he's not after a superficial spruce-up. He wants to dig deep, to get rid of the bad roots and the rocky ground so that we can live an abundant and fruitful life for him. He is passionate about our inner re-formation process. It is not that he does not love us as we are; it is that he knows our potential and he longs for us to be transformed. And God has given us a clear and compelling picture of what that transformation should look like. His name is Jesus. We are called to become more like Christ. Our primary identity as Christians is not to be church-goers or nice moral folk or even to be people who like quiche (although that is an undeniable added benefit); our primary identity is to be disciples – people who follow Christ, people who share Christ, people who through the Holy Spirit are becoming more like Christ. When digging into his word seems hard work, giving feels like hard graft, and the weeds of sin seem to keep tripping us up, we must fix our eyes on Jesus, who is the author and the perfecter of our faith (Heb. 12:2). He is the one who will motivate us and inspire us about the possibilities in our life, and who ultimately will transform us for eternity.

A High Price

Of course, transformation comes at a cost. When you wear a beautiful diamond, make no mistake, somebody some-where has paid a high price for you to own that beauty. It has cost somebody to buy it, but it has also cost others their time, their skill and a huge amount of hard work. Diamond mining, like gold mining, is a dangerous busi-ness. The workers are often badly paid, and sometimes even exploited. Despite the Kimberley Process (a cross-

God is asking us to join him in the process of transformation. government and industry set of guidelines to minimise the harm to people and the environment), it is widely understood that cor-ruption still exists, with many people still living in poverty as they find the precious met-als and jewels that we prize so highly.

After the diamonds are discovered and recovered there is still a long transformation process that takes place. This year my husband and I went to Amsterdam, which has been at the forefront of the diamond trading and cutting business since the sixteenth century. We spent a fascinat-ing afternoon visiting the renowned Coster Diamonds, where some of the most famous diamonds in the world have been painstakingly cut and shaped. We watched as stones were taken from rough to resplendent through the skill, accuracy and patience of the craftsmen working there.

We live in the knowledge that the ultimate cost of our transformation has already been paid by the sacrificial love of Jesus. He is not asking for us to do it all ourselves or to earn our own holiness points. He doesn't want to exploit our resources or leave us to shape ourselves. He is the one who makes transformation possible.

And he has not left us to work the ground alone. His Spirit joins us as we pick up our tools for the active and radical pursuit that is our discipleship. God is asking us to join him in the process of transformation. It might not always be easy and it will take time, but it is worth it.

The trouble is that we are a fast-paced instant gratification generation and we want our transformation now, and preferably without the digging bit. If we wait for more than an hour to receive an answer from a text message, we get twitchy. We want our shopping to be delivered by yesterday if you please. If possible we would love instantaneous spiritual maturity and flat-packed wisdom. But Christ-likeness is not a downloadable feature found on a handy lifestyle app, and we will all have to count the cost of living by faith. But it's not all down to us, and we are never alone. God makes transformation possible.

Love as Liberation

Every now and then I am reminded again of how passionately committed Jesus is to seeing us grow into all that we can be. When Jesus found fishermen, he looked beyond their nets and saw fishers of men. He knew that a dubious tax collector could become a generous party giver. Where others could only see problems, he saw potential. When he was presented with coal, he saw diamonds.

A few years ago now I came across a poem by Gerard Kelly that expressed this principle powerfully. Gerard and Chrissie are pioneers, authors and church leaders who, through their organisation Bless are a living example of how to serve others and polish the inner potential of people who may or may not always see their worth. I am grateful to them for the way they have blessed us personally and for this poem, which has spoken so powerfully to others as well as me.

We believe . . .
Every human being
has a worth worth seeing
Every name is a sound worth saying
Your potential a prayer worth praying
You see coal – God sees diamonds

We believe in the grace
Of the gifts God gives
His breath in everything that lives
Greater gifts to be discovered
Deep in you, disguised, dust-covered
You see coal – God sees diamonds

We see traces of truth
In the yearnings of youth

TRANSFORMED

God's image in imagination
We crave a community
That will honour audacity
And cherish the dreams of its children
You see coal – God sees diamonds

We see God seeking
A servant generation
Kindness as the kindling
To kick-start transformation
Love as liberation
Of a captive creation
We are digging
for the diamonds God sees

(Gerard Kelly
Used by permission)

This is the heart of our calling: to dig for the diamonds that God sees – in us and in others. We are asked to participate in the adventure of unearthing the potential treasure inside ourselves and to give permission to others to do the same. This is holy and liberating work. As Jesus tells us, 'Then you will know the truth, and the truth will set you free,' (John 8:32).

And that freedom matters. I recently read about a young female slave who, in 1853 in the Brazilian Bagagem mine, discovered an enormous diamond of almost 262 carats in its raw state. At the time, it was custom that anyone finding a significant diamond would be granted his or her freedom, and she was not only liberated but was also given an annuity for life from the mine owner. She was free indeed. The gem went on to be cut in Amsterdam. After the now famous Star of the South (128.48 carats cut) had been displayed at the Parisian World Exposition it was sold to the ruler of the Indian state of Baroda. It has most recently been purchased by the Parisian Jeweller Cartier.

But while the transformation and the life of that world-famous pink diamond was well documented, I wanted to know more about the slave girl who found it. Her life was defined by a discovery that would set her free. So what did she do with her freedom? Did she go on to have a fulfilling and long life? Did her new security change the trajectory of her family for generations to come? We will never know.

It seems to me that God's love liberates us like nothing else. Because of the price that Jesus has paid, we don't have to be captive to the things that have held us back up until now. We have no need to be slaves to sin or shackled to our past. We might have messed up forty-three times before breakfast today, but God never runs out of fresh starts and longs for us to live in the freedom of knowing that he has a future for us which is better and brighter than what has come before.

He sees the potential in us, and that truly is a liberating love. And he calls us to do likewise for others.

Transformed Transformers

A couple of years ago, I was invited to speak at an event where I had the pleasure of meeting a woman who was there to talk about her company called Rubies in the

Rubble. Jenny's story is inspiring. She saw the vast ocean of food that was being wasted in the food markets of London and felt compelled to act. She also saw the unfulfilled capacity in some of the capital's restaurant kitchens during the day and, significantly, she saw the untapped potential in some of the unemployed or disenfranchised people in the area and

There is some coal out there that God is asking us to see as diamonds.

decided that it had to be possible to do something significant for them. So Jenny gave up her highly paid job to begin an organisation that would make delicious chutneys, but that would also make the most of those gems that would have been wasted – the food, the facilities and the faces of people who needed a chance. She courageously followed her heart and applied her skills so that many unemployed and impoverished people have been given a fresh opportunity, creating chutneys that not only taste good but do good as well. Rubies in the Rubble's mission is 'to preserve, serve and to save' and it all came from the heart of a woman who listened to the whispers of God as he prepared her for a divine adventure.[11]

We all have the potential to bring hope to people and to places. You and I are called to deliberately walk away from the alleyways of despair and disunity, to discern where our efforts and energies can be best invested to make a lasting difference. There is some coal out there that God is asking us to see as diamonds.

[11]www.rubiesintherubble.com

Digging for DIAMONDS

I remember when my first daughter was very young, taking her into a video shop (remember those?) and being dismayed at the explicit and disturbing adult titles which were displayed on every shelf – some at the eye height of my toddler daughter in her pram. It was just sick and wrong. I expressed my concerns to the shop assistant, who predictably rolled out an exposition of policy and procedures and explained that titles were displayed alphabetically, meaning that there was little control over the height or placement of each individual title. Surely, I pleaded with him, he could see that this was a ridiculous policy which resulted not only in it being impossible for customers to find what they want but also possible to find what you really do *not* want in your face? The poor harangued assistant finally capitulated and said I should take it up with head office. So I did.

I cobbled together a petition of a few hundred signatures and wrote a polite but hopefully persuasive letter to one of the senior executives of this national chain of stores. Actually, I figured that senior executives are undoubtedly preoccupied and busy thinking about executivey-type stuff in boardrooms and that I would probably never hear anything again.

But I was wrong. A couple of weeks later I received a letter in the post (remember those?) inviting me to meet this very good man, who explained that he agreed with all I had written. He had been waiting for somebody to make the case from a customer's perspective in order to be able to instigate a change in policy, and he was delighted to inform me that they would now be displaying their videos firstly in genres – so you can go to the area of the store which has the kind of video you are looking for – but then also in age certificate with films for the youngest at the bottom and 18 certificate films at the top. And, not only would this be in my local store, but it would be rolled out nationally. Well, that was unexpected.

I appreciate that this shop is the tip of a very large iceberg. Now, through the Internet, deprivation and exploitation are a mere click away. But we have a choice to make in the face of the overwhelming tsunami of injustice, poverty, sadness and corruption that we face – we can give in or we can give more. There are things we can do. There are people we can serve. There are diamonds to be found in the least expected places. We must never be duped into thinking that one customer, one colleague or one constituent is powerless to create change. We must not accept the lie that things are as they are and they will always be that way. One person can change a community or a workplace. One person can start a charity or at least support one. One person can mentor or visit another person. Transformation is possible through any one person – and that includes you.

We can't eradicate every flaw and dark shadow of pain from the world but we have the privilege of joining with God in his desire to make all things new (Rev. 21:5). He longs to restore and recreate our environment and enable us to have a fulfilling and unblemished relationship with him. Until that final day when every tear is finally wiped away, we can join him in this transformative process. It will cost us something, but we are working alongside

Digging for DIAMONDS

those visionary men and women throughout history who believed that it was possible for slaves to be freed, for women to vote and for children to be immunised and fed. Those battles have not yet been won everywhere.

God knows that we are not able to transform everything but we can all transform something. We can't feed every hungry child but we can sponsor one. We can't create a nation of cohesive communities but we can get to know our neighbours and be hospitable. God is shaping us and placing us to play our part in his plans.

> God knows that we are not able to transform everything but we can all transform something.

God brilliantly designed coal to have the potential to become treasure. And you and I are packed with even more potential and travelling on a road towards transformation. God only knows what he can do through you. But along the road we will have the delight of discovering the treasure in us and unearthing the precious potential in others.

To see rubies in the rubble.
To dig for diamonds.
And to dream big dreams.

DIGGING DEEPER

- How does the realisation that diamonds are transformed coal spark your imagination?

- Why do we sometimes get distracted by more superficial transformation?

- Where has God transformed your life most powerfully or obviously and what digging needed to be done?

- How can you discover a more compelling vision of Christ that will motivate you in your journey of faith?

- What stands out most to you from Gerard's poem? Could you explore that further?

- How can we ensure we live fully in the freedom that Christ has won for us?

- How can you train yourself to see diamonds when you are immediately presented with coal? With people? With situations?

- Are there particular places, people or situations where you already feel compelled or called to bring transformation? How can you pray further into this and what steps can you take next?

All Powerful Creator God,

I thank you once again that nothing is impossible with you. I thank you for the work you have done in my life and the price that Jesus has paid for my transformation, here and for eternity. Lord, I pray that I will live a life compelled by a vision of you. I thank you that I can leave the past behind and live in freedom to serve you and to bring your life-changing power and hope wherever you call me. Lord, allow me to be a bringer of your transformation. Thank you that I have treasure in me to share and many more diamonds to discover.

In Jesus' transforming name I pray,

Amen

EPILOGUE

Dear reader,

If you are reading this now, and have therefore reached the end of this book, I would like to express to you my genuine delight (and some relief) that you have set aside time in your busy life to read and digest a book such as this. I have prayed for you as you have engaged with what would simply be ink on paper without a reader. May God bless you for investing so significantly in your inner life and outer purpose.

You and I have travelled some distance in these pages in a shared desire to grow stronger and deeper, and to look again at life as a project worth some serious spade-work, even as we rest in the knowledge that God is with us. This is not a contradiction, by the way. Our calling to be holy change-agents in our world, discovering treasure where others only see darkness, is not some kind of life-obstacle-course that we clamber through and climb over, feeling inadequate, alone and exhausted – it is an adventure which is possible because of the grace and resources of the One in whom we put our faith. We can know a peace beyond understanding because God is with us and for us, but he is also asking us to be passionately committed to playing our part in our own formation and in our world's restoration. Peace, passion and purpose, far from being mutually exclusive concepts, must work together as we rely on God but get stuck in to all he has for us.

As we wake up tomorrow morning and once again survey our countenance in the bathroom mirror, we will each consider the day ahead and we will also each have the liberty to choose our outlook: we can react to life as it happens to us in a defensive posture or we can respond positively to our life, engaging purposefully with everything around us. It is my hope and prayer that you now have a renewed commitment to responding in such a way that you will find and polish all that is valuable and of long-lasting significance, so that you might leave a legacy of immeasurable worth behind in this messy world.

Life is short. Surprisingly short. And as the years quietly slip by a day at a time, we are reminded that time really does fly. We can choose to focus on what is ultimately superficial, short-lived or self-serving, but deep down we all know that we are called to a grander vision and greater purpose in the moments that we are alive.

And while we might have to rummage a bit beneath the surface to discover all that God has in store, it is worth remembering again that carbon is ubiquitous. It is all around us. In fact, it is the fourth most abundant element in the universe (which I feel opens the gates for three potential sequels, *Haggling for Hydrogen*, *Ogling at*

Oxygen and the particularly hilarious *Giggling for Helium*. Step away from the keyboard, Cathy . . .). The point is that life would simply not be possible without the carbon that surrounds us everywhere and, likewise, sparkling insights and shining opportunities from God are not elusive or impossible to find, but the direction of our life depends on us identifying and owning them. Maybe, as Jesus said, what we need are the eyes to see and ears to hear what has already been revealed.

The problem is that it is perfectly possible for the things that are most familiar to us to begin to lose their power to amaze and captivate us. Do we, for example, occasionally forget to show how much we care to those whom we love the most? Might we overlook thanking God for the blessing of our homes or the beauty of the planet we inhabit? Do we, even, leave the Bible, full of endless wisdom and Spirit-inspired truth, up on the shelf where it cannot ever penetrate our heart, or forget to pray until we are desperate? Yes, it is possible from time to time to fail to see the value in what we have been given. But with God's help, we can do things differently today and start again tomorrow as well. With his power at work in us we can see the potential in the moments and circumstances that are, in very real ways, diamonds in our midst. Make no mistake – like carbon, they are always there.

The raw materials of our identity, our character, our strength and our purpose have been given to us by God, as have our experience and our relationships, and it is our responsibility to steward and protect them. Nobody else can do it for us. As I have written this book, I have been compelled to share that we all need to once again take ownership of the resources that God has given us and dig deeper into them every day, so that we can truly live the abundant lives of faith, hope and love that God has asked us to live.

Most of all, God assures us that as we seek him we will find him. He is always with us, and with the riches of his love to continually discover, we will always have more than we need – and enough to share with others.

So, let's be prepared to laugh out loud at ourselves but to take seriously the call of God on our lives. Together we can dig deeper than we knew was possible and discover that even in the messiness of everyday life, we are indeed richer than we had ever imagined.

God bless you.

Cathy

Twitter: cathymadavan
Facebook page: Cathy Madavan Speaker/Presenter/Writer
Website/blog: www.cathymadavan.com